The Ultimate Nordic Pole Walking Book

Klaus Schwanbeck

The Ultimate
Nordic Pole Walking Book

Meyer & Meyer Sport

British Library Cataloguing in Publication Data
A catalogue record for this book is available from the British Library

Klaus Schwanbeck – The Ultimate Nordic Pole Walking Book
Maidenhead: Meyer & Meyer Sport (UK) Ltd., 2009
ISBN: 978-1-84126-252-9

© 2009 by Meyer & Meyer Sport (UK) Ltd.
Aachen, Adelaide, Auckland, Budapest, Cape Town, Graz, Indianapolis,
Maidenhead, New York, Olten (CH), Singapore, Toronto
Member of the World
 Sports Publishers' Association (WSPA)
www.w-s-p-a.org

Printed and bound by: B.O.S.S Druck und Medien GmbH, Germany
ISBN: 978-1-84126-252-9
E-Mail: info@m-m-sports.com
www.m-m-sports.com

Contents

Acknowledgments

Writing this book has been a personal mission since I am convinced that a healthy lifestyle is not determined by sacrifice but by fun and friends. I hope this book will motivate everyone to become and stay physically active. This practical, scientifically founded advice is based on my 25 years of experience in the field of health sports.

Nordic Pole Walking is a wonderful, low-impact sports activity that anyone can do.

My slogan **Fun, Friends and Fitness** reflects the experience millions of pole walkers have made in the past years.

This book and the beginning of Nordic Pole Walking in Naples, Florida were only possible through the wonderful support of my wife Sabine. As sports physician and partner, she has made it possible for me to find many supportive friends in America.

Many of our American friends also supported me. I especially thank Heidi Klimt for her multi-level support and also as NPW-trainer, and Dr. Ekkehard Grampp, Chairman of the Board of NPWUSA, LLC, who worked 'around the clock' to help develop Nordic Pole Walking.

Also several organizations in Florida strongly supported my efforts: Both CEOs of NCH Health Care Systems in Naples, Florida, first Ed Morton followed by Allen Weiss, and both Managers of NCH Wellness Centers, Todd Monrad and Bobby Lee Gruninger, have energetically worked with me.

A VERY SPECIAL THANK YOU is due to our first 'Key Team' of NPW-Trainers — Sandi Davies, Angela Cohen, Pina Ohlsen and Carrie Robinson — who supported NPW with great enthusiasm, initiated the first NPW classes and helped to bring this wonderful sports activity into public awareness.

As an entrepreneur, I received tremendous support from volunteers of SCORE, namely Gray Poehler, Bob Anderson and Gregory Nelson, who opened many doors for me.

I am also so grateful for all Pole Walkers and friends in Naples and other parts of the U.S. who enjoyed this wonderful exercise activity like family and spread their experience to others with tireless enthusiasm.

I was very happy to quickly find business partners like Ray Marciano, CEO of Foot Solutions and Nancy Lazgin, Director of Worldwide Benefits of Staples, Inc. who both recognized the beneficial factors of NPW to the general population and integrated it into their businesses.

It's my vision to inspire as many Americans as possible to maintain a regular physical activity like Nordic Pole Walking.

Perhaps it is possible to convince American health insurance companies and health professionals to include NPW into their programs, as has been practiced in Germany for many years.

Who can walk – can also Pole Walk.

Nordic Pole Walking –
The Fastest Growing Trend Sport

Cross Country Skiers have known it for years … Millions of Walkers have experienced it for years…

Nordic Pole Walking and Exercise Walking are highly recommended low-impact exercises to improve fitness and health.

Nordic Pole Walking — one of the fastest growing outdoor sports activities — is a walking exercise anyone can perform. Using Nordic Poles is more beneficial than just walking without poles.

9

Why did Nordic Pole Walking become so popular in Europe?

Millions of Europeans quickly realized the additional advantages that are gained by Pole Walking. Walking without poles incorporates approximately 35 percent of all body muscles, while Pole Walking incorporates more than 90 percent of all your body muscles.

Perhaps you already know that cross-country skiing is one of the most efficient health sports to train your cardiovascular system and all body muscles at the same time. When cross-country-skiing, you smoothly glide on snow and push yourself forward by using leg, arm, and upper body muscles.

With Nordic Pole Walking, you perform nearly the same technique, but you wear your walking shoes instead of skies.

More than 50 percent of our muscles are located above the beltline, and Nordic Pole Walking involves all of them. When 90 percent of all body muscles are engaged, more than 600 muscles are working at the same time speeding up your metabolism. All upper body muscles become stronger and your cardiovascular-system is trained 25 percent more effectively in comparison to walking without poles.

Nordic Pole Walking requires no snow or skis, and you are not limited to winter seasons.

The good news for the broadest segment of the population:

On the beach or on the mountains, with Nordic Pole Walking you benefit from all these advantages at any time of the year, in any climate, or any terrain, without slipping and potentially falling like on slippery skiing trails.

Professional cross-country ski athletes recognized this 50 years ago. Walking and running with poles was used as summer-training to stay fit for winter competitions. By using poles, these athletes specifically trained their endurance and strengthened their leg, arm and upper body muscles.

Nordic Pole Walking is a form of walking that applies specially designed Nordic Poles to achieve a full body workout resulting in unbelievable results.

It is astonishing that the idea of Nordic Pole Walking for anybody's benefit was realized only ten years ago by Finnish athlete trainers.

"Whoever can walk – can Nordic Pole walk!"

Today in Europe, Nordic Pole Walking is more than just a trend – it's a broad movement. More than 10 million Europeans own Nordic Walking Poles. For example, health insurance companies in Germany contribute 80 -100% of the expenses involved for participation in Nordic Pole Walking classes that are conducted by certified NPW-instructors in fitness and health clubs, or for personal training.

Today, nearly 400 scientific studies and reports describe the tremendous health benefits and low risks of Nordic Pole Walking.

In the USA, Nordic Pole Walking is rapidly gaining in popularity – spreading from Naples, Florida all over the country. Our educated NPW instructors educate the public and create interest instantaneously when forming Pole Walking groups.

There is no other sports activity providing such great and immediate health & fitness benefits that is nearly risk-free and as easy to learn as Nordic Pole Walking.

When Nordic Pole Walking started out in Florida, we received remarks similar to the ones in Europe many years ago: Did you forget your skis? Are you looking for snow?

And the Floridians' answer was: "We need no snow."

Similar to what happened in Europe earlier on, Nordic Pole Walking became very popular in a matter of only a few months in Naples, Florida – now the "capital of Nordic Pole Walking in the USA." Seasonal visitors, called "snow birds," flocked to Pole Walking classes on the beach, became certified instructors, who then introduced Nordic Pole Walking to their northern home states.

With Nordic Pole Walking everybody benefits from the great potential of this exercise whether he/she is young or old, a "couch potato" or an ambitious fitness athlete.

A great outdoor sport - all year round

*Winter competition – cross-country skiing
and summer training*

History of Nordic Pole Walking 2

Nordic Pole Walking originated in Finland and dates back to the early 20th century. Cross-country skiers used their ski poles for snow-free exercise to stay in good physical condition during the summer months.

In 1985, Tom Rutlin, a cross-country skier and certified ski coach in the USA, experimented by adding rubber tips to his ski poles. His idea was to use the cross-country skiing pulling motion to engage the muscles of the upper body while fitness walking or running on an asphalt surface to strengthen the lower body muscles.

The term 'Nordic Walking' or 'Pole Walking' was born in 1997 when a Finnish ski equipment manufacturer, in cooperation with athletes and sports medicine experts, developed a fitness walking pole with an innovative wrist strap system. The wrist strap is the key component to the Pole Walking technique that allows walkers to perform the full range of motions that are associated with physical and health-related benefits.

Many physiological studies have confirmed that cross-country skiing is the most effective physical exercise for cardiovascular improvement and strengthening of all body muscles. Pole Walking emerged from cross-country skiing and has developed into a method of good physical exercise that is safe and effective for the general public, plus it is a social, enjoyable and stress-free activity.

Nordic Pole Walking USA has now brought this highly effective training and education system for physical fitness and mental relaxation to the United States, and it has already been adapted by people of all ages and all "walks" of life.

Nordic Pole Walking is fun and a very social activity.

It is ... Fun, Friends & Fitness ...

Health Benefits at a Glance

3

Meanwhile there are approx. 400 reports about (Nordic Pole) Walking in scientific & medical literature.

For example: In Germany, these studies are the basis for all German health insurance companies to pay 80% of the costs for a series of 10 Nordic Pole Walking classes conducted by certified instructors.

Health benefits/examples of scientific studies of Nordic Pole Walking:
- Nordic Pole Walking **burns up to 46% more calories** than exercise walking without poles or moderate jogging (Cooper Institute, 2004, Dallas and others).
- **Increases heart and cardiovascular training to 22%** more effect (Foley 1994; Jordan 2001, Morss et al. 2001; Pocari et al. 1997 and others).
- **Incorporates 90% of all body muscles** in one exercise and increases endurance of arm muscles (Triceps) and neck and shoulder muscles (Latissimus) to 38% (Karawan et al. 1992 and others).
- **Eliminates back, shoulder and neck pain** (Attila et al., 1999 and other).
- **Less impact on hip, knee and foot joints** about 26% (Wilson et al., 2001; Hagen 2006, and others)
- **Increase production of "positive" hormones.** Decreases "negative" hormones (R.M. Klatz et al., 1999; Dharma Singh Khalsa, 1997).

- Supports stress management and mental disorders (Stoughton 1992, Mommert-Jauch, 2003).
- Develops **upright body posture** (Schloemmer 2005).

Summary of all scientific studies

Nordic Pole Walking improves all parameters significantly – even though it is a low impact exercise !

3.1   Learn More about Health Benefits

Low impact exercising is your best health insurance. It is not the exhaustive training that keeps you healthy and fit. Many scientific studies show that there is a barrier when physical training begins to stress your body negatively rather than to improve your body's functions. When you train regularly up to a point at which you are really exhausted, your immune system weakens, more free radicals are produced, and your joints might be hurt.

Most sports activities workout only "half the body," like bicycle riding, walking or jogging. When using the Nordic Poles, you strengthen all your upper body muscles (see pictures below) and improve your cardiovascular-system at the same time.

Feel good and have fun

Nordic Pole Walking is the most effective total body wellness sport

It has been known for 50 years that cross-country skiing is the most effective physical exercise for cardiovascular improvement and total body muscle strengthening. Cross-country ski athletes have the best balanced physical results over all sports athletes.

Why leave these positive effects to a few athletes when everybody can accomplish the same – everywhere and anytime without skis and snow?

Advantages and facts:

There are a lot of advantages and facts that will motivate you to walk with your Nordic Poles:

Fat burning with this low impact sport

Nordic Pole Walking burns up to 46% more calories than exercise walking without poles or jogging with slow tempo, according to many scientific studies (Cooper Institute, Dallas, TX).

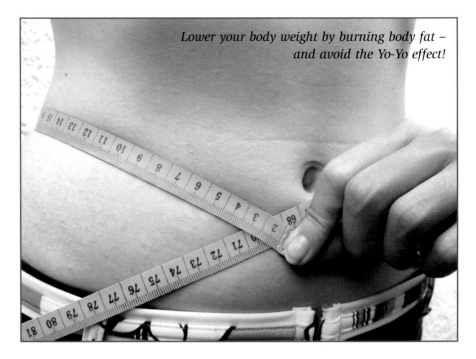

Lower your body weight by burning body fat – and avoid the Yo-Yo effect!

A weight loss diet without exercising your body does not work in the end. Your body is programmed for surviving. Not exercising means you reduce your metabolism. Your body stores calories as body fat for "expected" times with less food.

When doing a weight-loss diet with low calorie intake, instead of burning fat your body generates energy for muscle movement from stored glycogen in your muscles and can then attack your immune system. The scale shows you have lost pounds, when mostly you lost muscle substance and water – and, unfortunately, only very little body fat.

Shortly after finishing your diet, your body gains weight again, because your body still runs on a "low burning" program. According to this ancient program, your body stores nutrition into fat-deposits to be prepared for the next lack of food. This is the Yo-Yo effect.

If you want to lose weight you have to burn body fat. Fat in a considerable amount is only burned when muscles are working for a longer period of time and your heart beat frequency comes to an average of 120 – 140 beats per minute while exercising.

When sitting most of the day, walking from the parking lot to the office and back and so on, your body takes its energy from sugars (glycogen) stored in your muscles. Fat burning is not involved in this process since over time, our muscles 'unlearn' to burn fat due to losing their fat burning enzymes (S. Bartosch & H. Stengel, 2004).

After exercising 90 percent of your muscles with Nordic Pole Walking regularly for several weeks, you "re-animate" and rejuvenate your fat-burning process.

The good news is that you not only burn fat during your exercise, but when you relax after your Pole Walking session, your metabolism still continues burning body fat. This process is called "after-exercise burning" when your metabolism is still enhanced after your exercise for up to twelve hours.

Nordic Pole Walking impacts and changes the biochemical process in your body and you experience the following adaptation:

- Moderate growth of muscle mass

- Improvement of fat burning enzymes

- Improvement of mitochondria, the "ovens" in which fat is burned

- Improvement of mobilization of fat from the fat cells

- Improvement of metabolism (H. Stengel/S. Bartosch, 2004)

The next good news is: Pole Walking as a low impact exercise leads you nearly automatically to an exercise intensity-level called the "Fat Burning Zone" where you burn down most of your body fat.

Walk with 65 - 70% of your maximum heart beat frequency. For a healthy person this means 120 - 140 heart beats per minute. You can control this by measuring your pulse manually or with a pulse rate monitor you can buy in most sporting goods stores (read more in the chapter "Cardio Training"). This is a moderate but very effective walking tempo at which you feel comfortable and without a high impact on your joints.

For this reason, weight loss consultants and overweight people in Europe recognize Nordic Pole Walking as a great sports activity to burn body fat – and one which they really enjoy.

Naples, Florida April 2005: The "Pioneers" of Nordic Pole Walking in the Sunshine State

Some experiences from Pole Walking classes in Naples, Florida:

During our Wednesday Nordic Pole Walking classes, conducted by the NCH Wellness Centers in Naples, Florida, we measured the amount of calories burned with POLAR pulse rate monitors in each class on the same Pole Walkers every week for more than one year.

POLAR training monitors: measuring
• *Pulse rate*
• *Calories*
• *% Body fat, and more*

Our results matched existing scientific studies perfectly. We found that our Pole Walkers burned 800-950 calories during a 4.4 mile walk (1:10 h). At their weekly "spinning classes," they burned 500-600 calories in 60 minutes on spinning bikes, measured with the same POLAR pulse rate monitors.

In a step aerobic class, participants did 6,000 steps in 60 minutes. However, in a Nordic Pole Walking class they walked 7,500 steps (measured with pedometer) in the same amount of time with a burning rate of up to 800-900 calories. What great results!

At first, everybody was astonished about these large numbers of calories burned with Pole Walking. However, knowing that 90% of all body muscles are involved, these results are obvious.

For example, only 35% of all body muscles are involved when riding a bicycle or on a treadmill. A jogger incorporates only 65% of his body muscles. Pole Walking incorporates 90% + of all body muscles!

Activity	Percentage of body muscles involved (approximately)
Treadmill (bike)	35%
Jogging/Walking without poles	65%
Nordic Pole Walking	90% +

The simple explanation for the calorie burning rate with Nordic Pole Walking: *A working muscle burns calories. The more muscles you activate, the more calories you burn. That's one of the easy to understand "secrets" of Nordic Pole Walking*

Germany's health insurance companies support Nordic Pole Walking since the year 2000

In Germany, physicians recommend Nordic Pole Walking as a health sport. Most fitness centers, sports and health clubs offer Nordic Pole Walking classes. Within the last four years it has became a nationwide wellness program where everybody finds individual health benefits. Health insurance Companies pay 80% of the costs when participating in an instructional class for 3 months if conducted by a certified Nordic Pole Walking instructor.

This is a model for all other health insurance companies. Also Olympic athletes implement Nordic Pole Walking into their training as active regeneration training. More and more fitness enthusiasts use Nordic Poles while jogging as interval training and for advanced intensive physical training.

The technique is very easy to learn. We recommend joining a class with an instructor educated by Nordic Pole Walking USA or read the instructions in the chapter "Technique," very carefully; or order our DVD. You will experience the great benefits of this wonderful sports activity in a short time.

Less impact on joints

To move smoothly and without pain throughout your life, your joints need to be exercised. While jogging, each stride results in an impact of three times your body weight onto your joints. If you are a little overweight or over fifty years of age you should be careful not to harm your knee and hip joints. If you belong to one of these groups, a less-impact exercise like walking or Nordic Pole Walking is the better choice.

While walking, you always have one foot on the ground so your joints do not have to tolerate the hard impact of landing on the front foot heel. With Nordic Pole Walking, at the moment your heel touches the ground, your joints have to tolerate only the impact of your actual body weight. As biomechanical studies show, this is up to 30 percent less impact in comparison to jogging, when you perform a proper Pole Walking technique. With jogging one comes to a short "flying"-phase where both feet lose contact to the ground, and therefore, the impact upon "landing" on the front foot is much higher.

Roll your feet, use your Nordic Poles and strengthen your leg muscles

This is a great advantage in comparison to jogging, especially when you have to use paved inner-city sidewalks and trails, or for people after knee or hip surgeries or suffering from arthritis. Many people join Nordic Pole Walking after rehab, having a joint surgery or when suffering from arthritis. The Nordic Poles allow them to get back to a normal walking habit soon. The poles provide stability, balance and self-confidence for being able to walk for longer distance.

If you currently have or had a medical treatment on your knee or on your hip joints you should ask your health professional before you start training.

Arthritis is a wide-spread disease. Not exercising your joints will let them "dry out," movement becomes painful and leads to arthritis. When you are walking, your joints produce a "joint liquid" (synovial fluid) that guarantees a smooth joint-motion. This is what prevents arthritis and shortens the time of recovery after a surgery (learn more in the chapter "Prevent and Fight Arthritis").

Pain relief for neck, shoulder and back

Watch people and the common body postures around you. You often see slouched shoulders, hollow backs and rounded necks. People are talking about neck and back pain. When we feel stressed, we unconsciously raise our shoulders and tense shoulder and neck muscles.

A simple test will help you:
Remind yourself as often as possible to drop and relax your shoulders and straighten up your body posture. Every time you think of this and do it, you feel there is "room" for active body correction

As a result of a bad body posture and little workout your muscles get shorter, the discs in your spine dry out and your body posture gets worse. This results in pain in the upper spine region, tight neck and shoulder muscles, which can lead to chronic pain and headache. Instead of doing the right physical activity, the common solution is to pay a lot of money for medical treatments, physical therapy, massage therapy, acupuncture, and medication with all its side effects.

See the upper-body muscles which Nordic Pole Walking incorporates:

With Nordic Pole Walking you get your muscles fit again. You especially train your shoulder muscles, the upper and lower back muscles, the core muscles and even the abs and the chest muscles. You feel a good healthy tone in all these muscles and a better upright body posture.

A proper Nordic Pole Walking technique with its wide-arm swing, a good push onto your poles and a relaxed forward and backward rotation of your shoulders strengthen all these muscle groups as shown above.

People have told us that already after 3-4 Pole Walking sessions: "I lost my neck and shoulder pain; I can turn my head further back to the right and the left than I could do before."

This is the practice-experience that parallels all the medical studies.

Nordic Pole Walking is an effective "weapon" against muscle tension and neck and back pain.

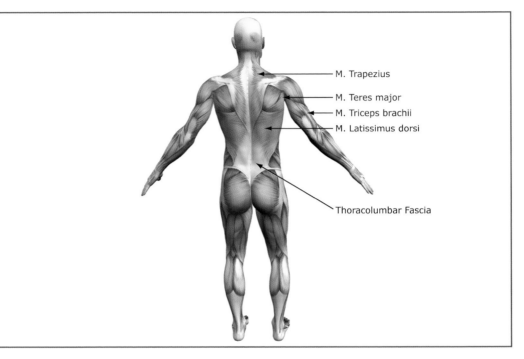

M. Trapezius

M. Teres major

M. Triceps brachii

M. Latissimus dorsi

Thoracolumbar Fascia

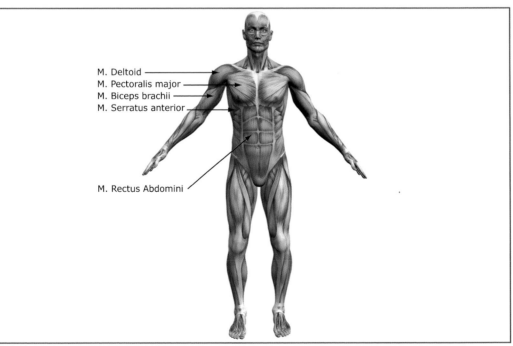

M. Deltoid

M. Pectoralis major

M. Biceps brachii

M. Serratus anterior

M. Rectus Abdomini

Your body is made for mobility. 75% of adults over the age of 40 suffer from back pain. Sitting and walking most of the day with rounded backs and slouched shoulders is against our body's needs. Back pain or pain in the joints tell us that they are not made for immobility.

Some examples:

- **Keep your muscles strong**

Muscles keep your body upright and are needed for each motion. To keep your muscles in proper function they need to be exercised. If not, your body works highly inefficiently.

Muscles degenerate because your body was taught by evolution to atrophy muscles which are not used in order to save energy and not to "waste" nutrition. For example, we experience these symptoms after having a leg in a cast, when muscle mass shows atrophy!

Your muscles support your joints and spine for stability and cushioning. Once they have gotten weak, there is no cushioning and stabilizing support anymore. All impact hits the cartilage, tendons and bones directly. This is a painful experience!

A former nice and upright body posture turns into a 'question mark position' with hollow back and rounded, slouched shoulders. The weakened muscles become tense and lead to back, shoulder and neck pain, and headache.
If you have experienced such symptoms lately, then it is time to get mobile again.

Nordic Pole Walking is the best and most convenient exercise for this!

- **Working the discs**

Get rid of back pain with Nordic Pole Walking!

The result of weakened back muscles often is a slipped disk. Tiny, deep lying muscles keep the discs in their position. The Nordic Pole Walking technique – rotation of spine and shoulders with each arm swing—keeps these muscles strong as well.

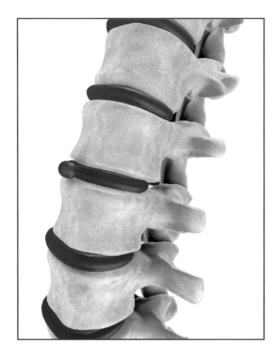

Another important fact is the nutrition of the discs:

Compare a disc with a sponge. With each walking stride, the slight pressure upon the disk squeezes the liquid out which feeds the disks with nutrients, and with the following relaxation-phase, the disk soaks the liquid inside like a sponge. So the disks are well-fed with nutrients they need.

Not exercising allows the disks to dry out. We cannot buy new ones like we can with a sponge – so we start to consult with a doctor.

Nordic Pole Walking can prevent this and does it for less money.

- **Strong and relaxed back, neck and shoulder muscles**

The same principle works for the big muscles of your back. By swinging the Nordic Poles and propelling yourself forward, all these muscles get stronger, and blood flows into your muscles. They relax after being fed with all the nutrients they receive from the blood flow. Last but not least, less suffering from headaches and pain from muscle tension is one of the great benefits of Nordic Pole Walking.

Learn special exercises in the chapter "A Total Body Workout".

Rejuvenation of hormones

Hormones influence your life significantly. They influence your moods and emotions. They determine your waking and sleeping rhythm, regulate your growths and "decrease" aging of all your body structure: muscles, cartilage, organs, skin, hair, sexual activity and more.

Stay biologically young

One of the main reasons for aging is the reduced production of hormones after the age of twenty five to thirty, like growth hormone, testosterone, DHEA and melatonin — the so-called "positive" hormones.

The good news is, as we know today, that you can stimulate your hormone production naturally and keep the level of "positive" hormones high by strengthening your muscles and through gentle endurance training like Nordic Pole Walking. Everybody knows people who physically exercise throughout their whole life and look much younger, stronger and are full of energy.

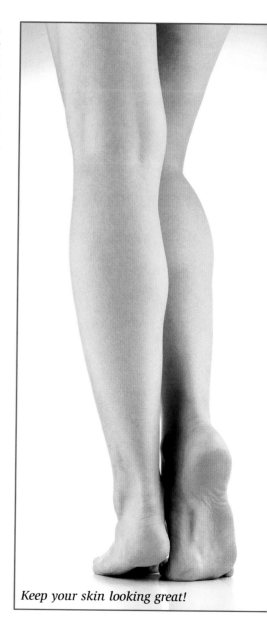

Human growth hormone (HGH), some call it the "Anti-Aging-Hormone," stimulates muscle growth, keeps vessels, cells and skin younger and strengthens your immune system. Testosterone makes you much more energetic, dynamic and powerful.

Nordic Pole Walking and "negative" hormones

Stress hormones are adrenaline, nor-adrenaline and cortisol. These hormones put your body into an alarm stand-by and guarantee the survival of the human being.

Positive stress keeps you moving forward and gives you motivation. Negative stress brings you down. Today, under the pressure of business, traffic and information-overload, we do not "work out" negative stress hormones like cortisol and the overdose on

Keep your skin looking great!

adrenalin. These stay in your blood circulation, increase blood pressure and damage your cells all over the body and brain. Therefore, we call these hormones "negative" hormones.

De-stress with Nordic Pole Walking and "burn down" these damaging stress hormones in your blood after your business day. If you exercise moderately in the morning, you built up protection and strength for the rest of day.

With only a one-hour walk or 30 minutes of Nordic Pole Walking a day three times per week, you avoid the age-related loss of muscles which starts at age 25 to 30 — a result of decreasing testosterone, DHEA and HGH levels.

Exercising with Nordic Pole Walking results in a higher production of positive hormones and reduces the production of negative hormones, like insulin, adrenaline and cortisol.

Cortisol is a stress hormone that produces glucose to prepare for physical activity. This is the same physiological mechanism which put our ancient ancestors into the status to fight or to escape from a dangerous situation. Today, you might suffer negative stress througout the day. Instead of starting a physical activity and burning the glucose as muscle energy, you might sit in your office, in your car or at home.

The unburned glucose is transferred into "fat reserves" in your abdominal area. This is not the case for regular Nordic Pole Walkers. They have a significant lower level of cortisol than people who do no regular physical exercise.

Insulin increases when your blood sugar increases, caused from eating too many carbohydrates or from stress as well.

The bad news:
Insulin lowers your blood sugar and without physical activity it turns into fat; Insulin also slows down the fat burning process.

The good news:
Nordic Pole Walking burns a large amount of fat (calories) and helps prevent insulin resistance and diabetes.

Enhancing the "Positive" Hormones and Neurotransmitters

Three times a week, for one hour or 30 minutes every day, Nordic Pole Walking produces a significant higher level of:

- Endorphin, which fights depression
- Dopamine for smooth moving and coordination
- DHEA, the "mother" of anti-aging hormones
- Estrogen, which fights osteoporosis, wrinkles, hair loss, sleeping problems and headaches
- Testosterone, which drives you forward, strengthens your muscles and libido
- HGH (Human Growth Hormone), which is responsible for muscle growth, increased bone density and less body fat
- Serotonin, which puts you in a good mood and reduces the appetite
- Acetylcholine, which improves your memory

Nordic Pole Walking 'lightens up' your brain

This message sounds strange, but it is a scientifically proven fact that regular physical exercise improves your brain's function. Let us have a look at the physiological process to understand how regular physical exercise influences your brain positively:

Pole Walking for only one hour three times a week, or 30 minutes every day, is enough to produce satisfactory cognitive improvements.

Your brain weighs only 2% of your body total weight, but needs 25% of your total blood supply. Nordic Pole Walking increases the amount of oxygen and glucose the brain receives. It tones the neurotransmitter system and increases the output of dopamine, acetylcholine, and endorphin for better body movement, memory and mood. It also increases the availability of brain-related enzymes, such as Coenzyme Q-10. It decreases low density lipoprotein, which clogs brain circulation to prevent strokes.

Nordic Pole Walking stimulates the production of your Nerve Growth Factor (NGF) – a virtual wonder drug for the brain. NGF supports the regeneration of your brain.

Nordic Pole Walking enhances the neuronal metabolism and improves your total energy exchange between your brain cells and the environment.

This energy exchange includes the exchange of oxygen, nutrients and cellular waste debris, primarily because Nordic Pole Walking improves blood circulation to the brain. This is beneficial for intelligence, learning ability, verbal fluency and cognitive ability.

Throughout human history it has been generally accepted that physical fitness benefits the mind. Plato, in 400 B .C, stated:

"A healthy brain needs a healthy body!"

Today, scientific studies prove Plato right:

Benefits of physical activity – burning extra 1,500 - 2,000 kcal
15 – 39% less coronary heart diseases
33% less stroke
12% less high blood pressure
12 – 35% less colon cancer
22 – 33% less breast cancer
18% less osteoporosis
(C. Diem, 2007)

Conclusion:

Nordic Pole Walking with its natural combination of endurance, strength, and mental training, and as social event as well, is a comfortable way to stay young and strong.

The Nordic Pole Walking Technique   4

The Nordic Pole Walking technique mimics your natural walking style with the support of two Nordic Poles. You walk and swing your arms as you walk every day. As the right leg moves forward, you automatically swing your left arm forward. There is no 'artificial' movement in the technique – you just walk naturally. When learning the technique, the goal is to perform all steps conscientiously and to get all movements well-coordinated.

After a short period of time, when your body is in "full swing," you will get the feeling of a natural, very comfortable and easy walking rhythm.

A hint for beginners: If you walk too slowly, you might not use your full arm swing. Walk at a tempo that feels comfortable to you.

Learn Nordic Pole Walking in 6 steps.

Follow these steps as described below and you will feel comfortable within the first few minutes.

Prepare your Nordic Poles:

a. The right length of your Nordic Poles

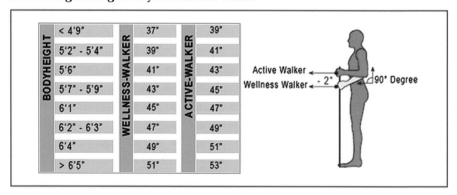

BODYHEIGHT	WELLNESS-WALKER	ACTIVE-WALKER
< 4'9"	37"	39"
5'2" - 5'4"	39"	41"
5'6"	41"	43"
5'7" - 5'9"	43"	45"
6'1"	45"	47"
6'2" - 6'3"	47"	49"
6'4"	49"	51"
> 6'5"	51"	53"

Active Walker
Wellness Walker — 2" — 90° Degree

When you start out, have your poles 1-2 inches shorter. As your technique improves, increase the length of your poles up to a 90 degree angle in your elbows. You will feel more resistance then.

If you have adjustable poles, adjust the poles to the optimal length for your body height.

Have your elbows and forearms in a 90 degree angle and drop your hands 2 inches down. Now, grip the poles. This is the best length for you to learn the technique = 65% of your body height. Then adjust the poles.

As soon as you feel comfortable walking with the poles, increase the length by 1 or 1.5 inches. With this length, your arm muscles will be involved more intensively. That's one of the advantages with adjustable poles.

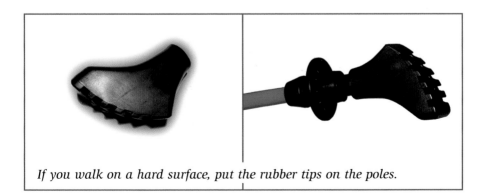

If you walk on a hard surface, put the rubber tips on the poles.

If you walk on a soft surface, remove the rubber tips.

Main Mistakes	Correction
1. Poles too long	Adjust grip 1-2 inches below elbow height
2. Poles too short	Adjust grip 1-2 inches below elbow height

b. The Nordic Pole Walking Hand-Loops – your power transfer to the Poles

Slip into the hand-loops as though you were shaking hands with the poles and adjust the grip to a comfortable fit.

To realize the purpose of the Nordic Pole Walking hand-loops, stretch both arms forward and open and close your hands. Your hands are always close to the grip.

Left: Hands closed: Comfortable NPW hand-loops

Right: Poles don't drop with open hands

Now you are ready to start.

Main Mistakes	Correction
1. Hand loops too tight	Loosen Velcro adjustment
2. Grips drop down more than 3 inches	Adjust hand loop tighter to grip

Six steps to the Nordic Pole Walking technique

Step 1: **Start walking with an upright body posture**

Put the poles behind your back and stand up straight and tall.

Stretch your shoulders back, raise your head up and look into the horizon, then relax your shoulders and drop them.

This is the perfect body posture Nordic Pole Walking will teach you. This is the posture you should maintain in your everyday life!

Now, start walking with your poles behind your back and concentrate on your upright body posture. Have your shoulders relaxed and your eyes focused on the horizon.

Poles held on your forearms behind your back force an upright body posture.

Step 2: **Start walking upright & naturally**

You start with an easy exercise:
Stand upright and keep your arms hanging loosely at both sides of your body. The tips of the poles are resting on the ground behind you.

Start walking and keep your body in a straight, upright position. Then begin swinging your arms slightly (as though you were walking without poles). Have your hands open and do not grip the poles – they are still connected to your wrists. The poles are now dragging on the ground behind you, following your arm swing.

Walk this way for 500 yards.

Main Mistakes Step 2	Correction
1. Slouched shoulders	Straighten up
2. Looking to the ground	Eyes to "horizon"

Drag your poles & start walking

Step 3: Increase your walking speed and arm-swing

Swing your arms & still drag your poles with open hands

Swing your arms a little more. Like walking, your right arm swings forward when your left leg moves forward, and vice versa. You don't need to think about it – just walk. The correct movement is embedded into our genes.

In case you find this natural cross-coordination difficult to perform, because you focused too much on your arm and leg motion, or started out by swinging your RIGHT arm and moving your RIGHT leg forward at the same time – just start over again with Step 2 above. You will have solved this 'problem' in just a few minutes.

- Keep your hands open, walk upright and relax.

- By walking a bit faster, you will feel a slight resistance from your poles in your hand-loops when the pole-tips grip slightly on the ground.

- Walk relaxed for another 500 yards. Stay with your arm swing rhythm.

- Stay upright and relax.

- You feel yourself walking upright ("proud") in a natural walking style.

Walk relaxed & upright

Main Mistakes Step 3	Corrections
1. Arm swing not coordinated	First step with opposite foot front
2. Slouched shoulders	Look to the "horizon"

Step 4: Learn to push your poles

Now, grasp the handle of your left pole at the same moment your right foot touches the ground in front of you and push the pole strongly into the ground. Continue vice versa.

With pushing the poles, you will instantly feel how the resistance to your arm and shoulder muscles increases. Because of the Nordic Pole Walking hand-loops you don't need to clutch the grips very tightly. Keep your muscles relaxed.

Your arm-push is the key to success:

By using the poles to propel yourself forward, you really actually achieve all the benefits of Nordic Pole Walking by enhancing energy consumption of up to 46% in comparison to just walking exercise.

The difference that makes a good Pole Walker happens when the push onto the poles comes from your shoulder joints (not from the elbow joints). You perform a good perfect Nordic Pole Walking motion with your shoulder rotator joints.

Your arm swings forward from your shoulder joint. Your elbow is slightly bent. The poles are "hanging" attached to the hand-loop while your fingers grasp the pole-grip slightly with your muscles relaxed.

At the end of the forward swing, your hand grasps the pole-grip and you push the pole (from your shoulder joint!) backwards to the ground.

The tips of your poles always face backwards - they are never in front of your body!

Your arm pushes backwards with a slightly bent elbow and feels the resistance of the pole when pushed to the ground. Push back as far as possible without losing your walking rhythm. Then your hand loosens the grip and opens up slightly.

See the motion in the shoulder joint.

Push backwards and relax hands at the end of the swing

The correct walking rhythm is to clutch the pole-grip at the end of the forward arm swing and loosen the grip (open your hand) after pushing the pole when your hand had pasted your hip while swinging back.

This way, your triceps, biceps and forearm muscles get an extra workout.

Now, keep walking for approximately 30 minutes and experience the power of your poles. You are walking with a straight, upright body posture at a comfortable speed – not too fast and not too slow.

Having achieved this step to perform the technique, you will feel wonderful. You have now experienced the feeling of what Nordic Pole Walking will do for you.

You can stop after Step 4 as the completion of your first Nordic Pole Walking training. You have achieved the basic Nordic Pole Walking technique.

Congratulations – you have done very well! – Enjoy!

You can now work on Steps 5 & 6 at your next Nordic Pole Walking training session to improve your technique.

Main Mistakes	Correction
1. No "push" to the ground	Close hands; feel resistance from "push" in arms and shoulders
2. Hands too tense on grip	Relax hands at the end of backswing

Step 5: Walk with a slight & relaxed shoulder rotation

After becoming familiar with Nordic Pole Walking, you are ready to involve all of your upper body muscles into the technique.

Start walking as you did before for about a mile. Remember to walk with a straight, upright body posture and a comfortable, easy walking rhythm.

Now, relax your core-muscles and incorporate a slight forward and backward rotation of your shoulders with the rhythm of your strides.

The shoulder of your opposite leg always swings forward and the shoulder over the forward moving leg swing backwards – just as the natural way of walking. Practice this every time. This rotation will keep you in balance. With the back swing out of your shoulder, swing your arm as far back as it is comfortable for you (see picture).

When you are a novice Nordic Pole Walker, it is important that you conscientiously

Walk naturally. Your shoulders slightly rotate forward & backward

complete these rotations every day, so that all core and back muscles, even the deep-lying back muscles close to your spine, are involved and strengthened.

With each stride, keep moving in a slight and very conscious rotation of the upper body and you will realize that your whole body is in a relaxed, comfortable walking swing and rhythm.

Keep walking for another half or full mile and concentrate on the upright body posture and the upper body swing rotation. Walk naturally and relaxed.

After a short time, you will be familiar with this full body movement and it will just become natural to you.

Increase your walking speed

NOT CORRECT:
Do not reach out with strides

Increasing your walking speed begins with a stronger backward-push from your shoulders to your poles.

'Your arm and shoulder muscles are the > engine < which propel you forward'. The harder you push, the more your poles propel you forward. Your strides become a little longer automatically.

Do not reach out with your front leg to extend your stride. Your strides get longer naturally by pushing the poles. Reaching out too far in front leads to a stretched (locked) knee at the very moment your heel touches the ground (picture 1). Don't 'march' or walk like a soldier. This places more pressure on your knees.

Rely on your poles. When doing it correctly, your knee is naturally slightly bent with the touchdown of your heel to the ground (picture 2). This reduces the impact on the knee and hip joints by up to 30%.

CORRECT:
Walk naturally

Main Mistakes Step 5	Correction
1. Over rotation of shoulders	Swing shoulders slightly with walking rhythm
2. No shoulder rotation	Swing shoulders forward & backward with walking rhythm
3. Problems coordinating shoulder	Walk faster; rotation develops naturally

Step 6. Improve your Pole Walking technique

a. The arm swing

To incorporate more shoulder muscles, swing your arm forward with a slightly bent elbow. Picture yourself "shaking hands" with somebody far in front of you (Picture 1).

Keep this arm position while swinging back and pushing your poles (picture 2).

Advantage: Now you feel that the push originates not from the elbow motion, but from your shoulder. Your shoulder rotator muscles do the job.

Pushing the poles "from your shoulders" incorporates triceps and shoulder muscles & reduces impact on knee & hip joints.

1. "Shaking Hands" position

2. Your arm swings back from the shoulder joint

Grasp grip when pushing –
Open hand when back-swinging

b. Train your forearm muscles

At the end of the forward-swing, grasp the pole-grip and open your hand as soon as you pass your hips while swinging back.

Advantages:

a) You train your hand and forearm muscles.

b) You relax your arm and shoulder muscles with each stride.

Roll your feet consciously from heel to toes

c. Roll your feet consciously

Never have a locked knee when your heel touches the ground!

As your heel touches the ground, your knee is slightly bent automatically. Then roll your feet from heel to toes. Picture squeezing a lemon with your sole.

Advantages:

a) You touch the ground softer and have less impact on your knees.

b) You work your calf and shin muscles.

Main Mistakes Step 6	Correction
1. Swinging poles from the elbows only	Keep arms "long" while swinging
2. No "swinging-movement" in shoulders	Swing slightly bent arm from "shaking hands" position backward
3. Problems with opening and closing hands	Start exercising with one hand
4. Locked knee with too long a stride	Roll feet consciously from heel to toe

Great Job! – CONGRATULATIONS !

As you realized, it takes some coordination to perform the correct Nordic Pole Walking technique. It is not difficult to achieve and enjoy all the benefits by performing the correct technique.

You might see other Pole Walkers who do not use their Poles correctly, e.g. just drag their poles and not push them.

But you make the difference!

It's the same as in other sports activities: learning and performing the correct technique results in increased fun and success.

Nordic Pole Walking is the ideal exercise for anybody

5 A Total Body Workout

Nordic Pole Walking is not only about walking with Nordic Poles – it is a total body workout for everyone. Either individually, with a partner or with a group. You can use the poles for:

A. Breathing exercises

B. Mobilization exercises

C. Stretching exercises

D. Strengthening exercises

E. Flexibility exercises

Being able to exercise outdoors is one of the great advantages of Nordic Pole Walking. Exercising in fresh air, socializing and having fun are enticing factors to make Nordic Pole Walking part of your daily routine.

The following chapter features a sequence of exercises from A to F. It is suggested that you perform these exercises in the order given as a warm-up program before starting your walk. Choose one or two of the examples featured below. There are many more that will be demonstrated and taught by your certified instructor.

A. Breathing exercises

Deep breathing helps you before the early morning training to increase oxygen in your blood and to "wake up."

As an after-work exercise, it helps you to calm down from daily stress and get into balance for an enjoyable and relaxing walk.

Exercise 1: "Swing your poles smoothly from right to left"

(1) Stand relaxed and upright.
(2) Lift both poles with both hands horizontally to the front of your chest.
(3) Rotate your upper body from right to left and inhale deeply.
(4) When swinging back, exhale as thoroughly as possible.

Complete 10 repetitions.

Exercise 2: "The Thai Chi"

(1) Hold both poles together on each end and stretch your arms straight above your head while bending your knees slightly.

(2) Take a deep breath and bend down slowly from the waist, while exhaling thoroughly.

(3) Rise up slowly with your poles moving up close to your body and inhale deeply.

(4) Stretch your arms and poles toward the sky and repeat.

Complete 5–10 repetitions.

B. Mobilization exercises

Since all of your joints are engaged when Nordic Pole Walking, it helps to stimulate your joints.

Exercise 3: "Swing your legs"

Bend (mobilize) your knees while swinging forward.

(1) Place both poles in front of you for balance.

(2) Swing your right leg forward and backward.

(3) Stand as upright as possible.

(4) Be sure you are bending your standing knee while swinging forward and stretching backward.

With this simple exercise, your hip and knee joints begin producing "joint-liquid" and the tendons become flexible.

Complete 10 repetitions with each leg.

Exercise 4: "Cross-swing your legs"

(1) Use both poles for balance with forward stretched arms.
(2) Swing your right leg from right to left behind your poles.

This enhances the flexibility of your hip tendons.

Complete 10 repetitions with each leg.

*To the left and
to the right*

Exercise 5: "Raise your heels"

(1) Placing your poles in front for balance, have your body weight on your heels.
(2) Stand in an upright position (good posture!).
(3) Roll from your heels to your toes by lifting your heels, then roll back to your heels.

Complete 10 repetitions.

Body weight on heels rolling to toes

Exercise 6: "Kayaking"

Turn the upper hand down at the end of the swing – like kayaking

(1) Standing upright, hold your poles like you would hold a Kayak paddle with both hands.

(2) Start "paddling" from the right side, rotating your upper hand back & down with your lower hand moving up.

(3) Rotate your poles over to the left side and repeat as above.
Swing the "paddles" by rotating your upper body as far back as you can.

Start slowly. This exercise mobilizes all your shoulder muscles.

Complete 10 repetitions.

C. Stretching exercises

Stretching exercises strengthen and stretch your muscles at the same time.

Exercise 7: "Stretch your calves, hamstrings and gluteus"

(1) Place your poles in front for balance and take a long stride forward with your right leg.

(2) Lift your toes, so the front leg is stretched.

(3) Shift your weight to your left leg stretched out in the back. You will feel a slight stretch on the backside of that leg.

(4) Hold this position for 30 seconds.

(5) Switch the left leg to the front position and repeat the exercise.

Complete 2 repetitions with each leg.

Exercise 8: "Stretch your quadriceps"

(1) Hold both poles in your left hand for balance.

(2) Lift your right foot to your back and try to hold it with your right hand. You will feel a slight stretching in your quadriceps.

(3) Hold this position for 30 seconds.

(4) Repeat with your left leg.

Complete 2 repetitions with each leg.

Stay upright and pull your foot to your buttocks.

Exercise 9: "Stretch your adductors"

Shift to the left

Shift to the right

(1) Placing your poles in front for balance, step sideways with your left leg.

(2) Shift your body weight to your left leg while bending your knee.

(3) Keep your right leg stretched out sideways with your foot flat on the ground. You will feel a slight stretching in your right adductors.

(4) Hold this position for 30 seconds, then shift your body weight to your right leg and repeat the same stretching with your left leg.

Complete 2 repetitions with each leg.

Exercise 10: "Stretch your hip flexors"

Shift your front knee forward over your toes

(1) Place your poles in front for balance and take a long stride forward with your right leg.

(2) Shift your pelvis forward, bend your front knee and lean back slightly. You will feel a slight stretch in your hip.

(3) Hold for 30 seconds.

(4) Repeat this exercise with your left leg in the front position.

Complete 2 repetitions on each leg.

Exercise 11: **"Stretch your shoulder, back and arm muscles"**

Stretch left arm forward *Stretch right arm forward*

Bodyweight on your heels & alternately shift your poles as far forward as you can.

(1) Place your poles in front for balance, lean your upper body forward and stretch both arms out as far as you can.
(2) Relax & bend your right arm slightly and stretch your left arm forward. Hold for 10-30 seconds.
(3) Repeat the same stretch with your right arm. You will feel a good stretch in your shoulders, back and arms.

Complete 2-5 repetitions with each arm.

D. Strengthening exercises

Exercise 12: "Parallel squats"

Sit down on an invisible chair

(1) Using your poles in front for balance, hold your back straight and remain in a good body posture.

(2) "Sit down" in an invisible chair. Move down and up slowly.

Complete 10 repetitions.

Exercise 13: "Stride squats"

Stride Position   Kneel down – Rise up   *Rise up – keep upper body erect*

(1) Place your poles in front for balance, stand upright in a comfortable stride-position with your right leg put forward.

(2) Bend your left, stretched back leg down as far as you can and then rise up again.

(3) After 10 repetitions, switch your legs, putting the left leg in front, and repeat the exercise.

Keep your upper body erect during this whole exercise.

Complete 10 repetitions with each leg in front.

Exercise 14: "One-leg-squats"

Standing and bended knees

(1) Use your poles for balance.

(2) Cross right ankle over your left knee.

(3) Bend left leg as low as you can.

Complete 5–10 repetitions.

Exercise 15: **"Isometric arm & shoulder strengthening"**

(1) Stand upright and hold the poles horizontally in front at shoulder-height.

(2) Tightly hold the poles on both ends and pull your right hand to the right and your left hand to the left (as though you would try to pull the poles apart).

(3) Hold tightly for 30 seconds.

(4) Relax and hold.

(5) Tightly hold your poles again and press toward the middle of the poles without sliding your hands. Press for 30 seconds. You will feel your arm and shoulder muscles contracting.

Complete 2–5 repetitions each.

Exercise 16: **"Isometric triceps strengthening"**

(1) Stand upright and tall. Hold your poles vertically behind your back.

(2) Tightly grip the bottom ends of the poles with your right hand behind your waist and the top end of the poles with your left hand behind your head.

(3) Pull your left hand upward and your right hand downward. Hold this position for 10 to 30 seconds.

(4) Relax and hold.

(5) Tightly hold the poles again and press toward the middle of the poles without sliding your hands. Hold for 10 to 30 seconds. Keep inhaling and exhaling.

You will feel a strong contraction in your triceps.

Each arm 2-5 repetitions.

Exercise 17: "Strengthening your back muscles & gluteus"

(1) Place your poles in front for balance, lean your torso forward and put your body weight on the right leg.

(2) Lift your left leg straight backwards and stretch up as far as possible. Hold this position for 10 to 30 seconds.

(3) Switch legs with your body weight now on your left leg while stretching your right leg as described above.

You will feel contraction in your back muscles and gluteus.

Complete 5 repetitions with each leg.

Exercise 18: "Push-ups with the poles"

This is a partner exercise.

(1) One partner kneels on one leg and stretches both poles horizontally behind the neck, pushing up slightly.

(2) The other partner is standing behind the kneeling partner and grips the poles with both hands from above.

(3) The standing partner slightly pulls the poles upward while the kneeling partner pulls the poles downward.

(4) Then partners change positions and repeat.

Complete 2 sets of 10 repetitions.

E. Flexibility exercises

There is no need for you to practice extreme exercises.

Flexibility and stretching enhance the moving range of your joints, stretch your muscles and keep tendons flexible.

As an example, back pain is often a result of lack of flexibility. When you are not exercising your hip flexors, they shorten and tense up, eventually pulling your pelvis forward.

The result is continuous tension on your back muscles and continuous pressure on your discs in the lower back region.

Therefore, stretching the hip flexors is a recommended exercise, as demonstrated in the pictures below.

Stretch hip flexors

Stretch your gluteus

Keeping and enhancing the flexibility of your spine should be a daily exercise.

Bending forward down   *Bending sideways*   *Cross your feet*

Turn your shoulders from the right to left and vice versa

Shoulder flexibility

Grasp your poles behind your back and lift your arms up as far as you can

Grasp your poles and stretch your arms bending forward. "Push" your chest downward

You feel great!

6 Criteria to Buy the Right Equipment

Your basic equipment

As with any other sports activity, it is crucial to have the right equipment. Before you are going to buy your poles, walking shoes etc., we suggest that you familiarize yourself with the necessary equipment.

1. The Nordic Poles
2. Walking shoes
3. Functional sportswear
4. Drink belt/ Fanny Pack
5. Hat/Cap to protect against sun or to protect against the cold

Once you walk regularly and have determined your personal goal, we recommend these additional accessories:

6. Pedometer or a pulse rate/calorie-watch
7. Gloves (for colder seasons)
8. Global Nordic Pole Walking website to track your success (gnpwalking.com)

6.1   The Nordic Poles

Material:

Your poles, of course, are the most important tool you need for Pole Walking. It is the ultimate sports equipment, which has to fulfill special requirements. To avoid stress on wrists, elbows or shoulders, you should not use skiing or trekking poles.

The nordic poles are made of carbon or a carbon-fiber mixture. The upper part of the adjustable poles is made of aluminum and the lower part is made of carbon. These materials guarantee the best stability, lightness and flexibility and soften the impact on your arm and shoulder joints.

A high quality nordixx-Pole should offer:

- Support
- Tracking
- Cushion

The harder the pole material, the more the impact affects your arm and shoulder joints. Stiff, but flexible materials, plus a balanced Nordic Pole construction absorb most of this impact.

The optimal pole length is 0.65 % of your body height. To measure this, stand upright with a 90-degree angle in your elbow, and—for the beginner—drop your forearm down by 2 inches.

The advantage of adjustable poles is that you can change them to a length that is most comfortable for you.

After you have walked with the 2-inch dropdown in height for some time and your technique has improved, you may try to increase the length of your poles.

You also may want to adjust the poles when walking on soft surfaces like sand where the poles sink in about 2 inches, or for your walk on asphalt with the rubber tips slipped on.

The chart below is a basic recommendation for the correct pole length to start out with. Later, as a more experienced walker, you can adjust to the length that feels best for your personal walking style.

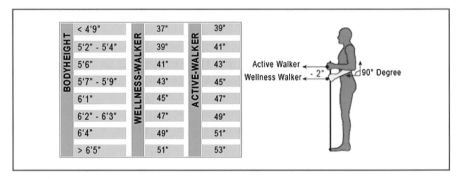

BODYHEIGHT	WELLNESS-WALKER	ACTIVE-WALKER
< 4'9"	37"	39"
5'2" - 5'4"	39"	41"
5'6"	41"	43"
5'7" - 5'9"	43"	45"
6'1"	45"	47"
6'2" - 6'3"	47"	49"
6'4"	49"	51"
> 6'5"	51"	53"

Active Walker
Wellness Walker - 2"
90° Degree

The hand-loops:

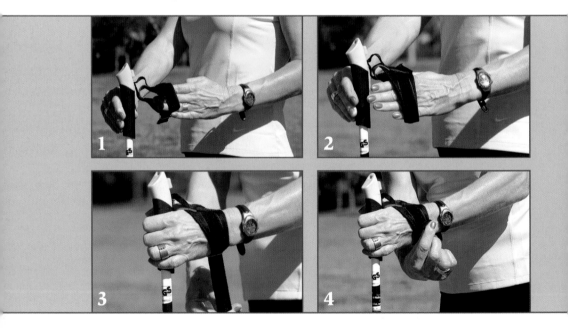

Specially designed hand-loops for walking permit optimal transfer of the forward-propelling pushing power that comes from your arms and upper body onto the poles.

In contrast to Nordic Poles, the hand-loops of hiking or skiing poles do not allow your hand to open while swinging back.

With the nordixx hand-loops, it's not necessary to hold the pole grip tightly during the arm swing, because your hand is kept close to the pole grips all the time.

Before purchasing your poles, make sure that you can open and close your hands completely during exercise.

Try the poles and see whether you feel comfortable with them. The hand-loops should be manufactured of soft (not a stiff) material. This prevents blisters between your thumb and forefinger. The material for the grip should be sweat-absorbing (EVA) and should be able to be cleaned easily like the grips of the nordixx-poles.

A very comfortable grip-system is available so that you can detach from the poles with a "click". This frees your hands for drinking, binding shoe laces, etc.

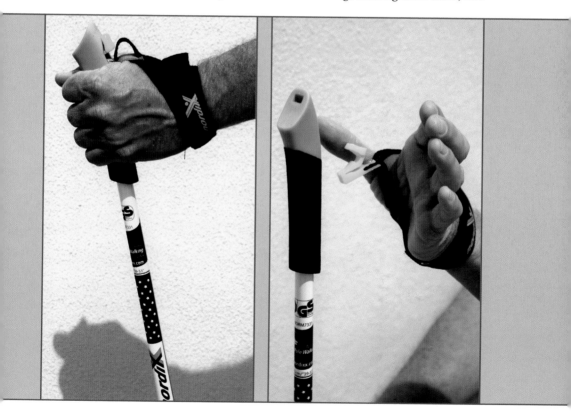

The nordixx "Free Hand"

The tips of your Poles

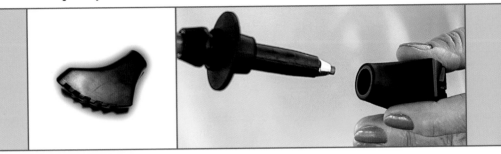

When you Pole Walk on a hard surface like asphalt, put your rubber tips on the pole tips. There are different sorts of hardness for rubber tips:

The softer the rubber tip, the better your traction on asphalt, but these soft rubber tips wear out relatively fast. However, don't use rubber tips that are very hard. Although they last longer, the traction is not very good.

The nordixx rubber tips are a proven compromise between long lasting and good traction.

When walking on soft surface (forest trails, grass, beach etc), take the rubber tips off. The poles have blunt carbide steel tips, which provide optimal traction. Buy poles that don't have sharp steel tips to prevent injuring yourself or somebody else. There is no real advantage in using sharp pole tips.

Nordic Walking shoes

Shoes for sports are often considered not very important. Knowing that our feet hold our total body weight, they can be compared to the foundation of a house: If the foundation is not well-balanced, it will result in cracks in the walls. In terms of our bodies, it hurts our joints, tendons and spine.

For our daily lives and especially in sports where you have more impact on your feet-"foundation," look for good walking shoes and, if necessary, customized insoles.

Walking shoes, other than running shoes, should have a relatively flat and rounded heel other than running shoes. This helps you to stay upright and increases the strength in your calf muscles, hamstrings and gluteus.

The rounded shoe heel guarantees that your heel touches the ground flat and complete. That is not the case with running shoes. The heel is higher, because running has a different foot motion. The middle part of the shoe should be stable but flexible to avoid rolling of your feet to the outside (supination) or to the inside (pronation). You don't need this extreme cushioning for walking shoes.

6.2   Criteria for Walking Shoes

When you buy your walking shoes consider the following recommendations:

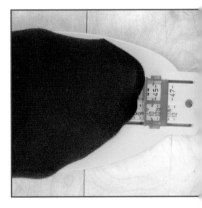

- Buy your shoes at least $1/2$ a size or even 1 size larger than your dress shoes

- When rolling your feet from the heels to the toes, toes need space in the shoe front. This way, you avoid blisters and contusions on your toes. Therefore, the shape of a good walking shoe is wider in the front.

- The sole in the shoe's front part should be very flexible in the rolling direction and stable in the middle to avoid supination or pronation.

- The original insole should be removable in order to replace it with a custom-made insole.

- Your heel should be held comfortably by the shoe's shape.

- A good sporting goods shop or sports shoe shop carries different widths of walking shoes. Ask the service people for the proper fit.

- A good specialized shoe shop first measures your foot size, and then computerizes your foot shape and sole.

6.3   Functional Apparel

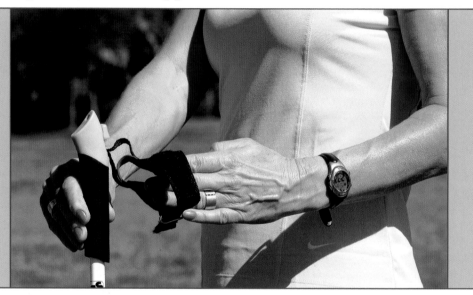

"Wick-away" – is a slogan for active peoples' sports clothes. Common cotton underwear absorbs sweat like a sponge and keeps it wet. It dries slowly and can result chilling your body. Modern microfibers transport your sweat to the outside of the fabric where the moisture vaporizes, keeping your skin much drier and warmer.

The material you should look for:

- Polypropylene
- Polyester
- Poly-acrylics

Brand names include Coolmax, dryfit, Gore-Tex and others.

Some products promise to absorb moisture, be waterproof and windproof. Product tests have shown that these multifunctional materials often do not wick sweat away outside as promised.

The best solution is to be dressed in the "onion-principle":

Depending on weather conditions, wear your clothes like onion skins: T-shirt, sweat-shirt and rain-jacket (Gore-Tex) made of microfibers. Put one over the other, and you have the ability to pull off a "skin" when it gets too hot.

Don't forget to protect your head from the sun or cold weather, and wear a cap. You probably know that in cold weather, most of your body heat is "lost" through your head.

Keep your hands warm in the winter and wear gloves. There are special Nordic Pole Walking gloves or cross-country gloves available, made of microfiber to keep hands warm and dry.

The same principle applies to your feet: Buy socks which transport moisture to the outside and keep your feet dry and warm.

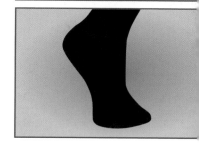

6.4   Drink Belt / Fanny Pack

In order to drink while you work out, it is recommended you wear a so-called "drink bottle belt" or fanny pack to carry a water bottle.

When you buy one, make sure it wears comfortably. Look for a model with a broad belt which does not impact your back with each stride.

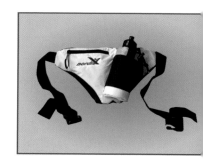

It should have additional pockets for a snack if you walk longer, your keys and cell phone. We also recommend having your business card and a piece of medical tape with you.

Diabetics should also have some pieces of hard candy in their fanny pack. People with heart disease are advised to carry along their 'emergency medication' – just in case.

6.5 Additional Equipment

Pedometer

As described in the chapter "Cardio Training," use a pedometer to measure the amount of steps, miles and calories. Pedometers are not as precise as a good heartrate and calorie monitor.

When you buy a pedometer look for the following functions:

- Step counter
- Odometer/mileage counter
- Caloric counter
- Easy to read in sunshine

We recommend pedometers which allow downloading of your data into your computer to evaluate your training.

Heart rate and calorie monitor

High quality monitors have software to calculate your optimal training zone (O-Zone), heartbeats and amount of burned calories. They have an interface to store your data in your computer.

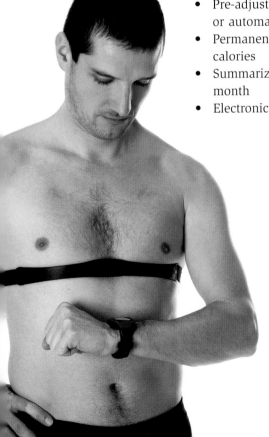

- Storage of your biometric data (gender, age, weight, height)
- Pre-adjustment of your training zone manually or automatically
- Permanent display of actual pulse rate and calories
- Summarizing data per training session, week, month
- Electronic shoe clip to measure distance

7 Weight Loss with Nordic Pole Walking

Sustainable weight loss with Nordic Pole Walking

A question we hear frequently: "How long and how often per week do I have to pole walk to lose bodyweight?"

This chapter gives you a substantial background and a simple formula to achieve the amount of body fat you want to lose. Fill out the formula and you will know how many hours per week you have to pole walk.

Additionally, you should control or reduce your calorie consumption from food.

Combine Pole Walking with controlled nutrition and you will experience a new quality of life!

This weight loss strategy without a Yo-Yo Effect brings you a healthy and enjoyable lifestyle step-by-step, and you won't miss what you like to eat or drink.

As Paracelsus, an early physician, who lived from 1493-1541, claimed: "It's the dosage, which makes the difference." (see: BERLIN Weight Loss Concept).

This is not a diet for a limited time where you lose weight – and gain weight again (sometimes more than you had before) as soon as the diet ends.

Step-by-step you will learn how to reduce calories. You can eat nutrient dense foods that are enjoyable while at the same time consuming less calories.

You eat and burn calories. Your calorie intake and calorie burning stay in balance after you have achieved your target body weight (learn more in chapter 15 "A Great Tool to Change Your Lifestyle").

How to make this balance visible?
You learn to use four tools:
1. Calculate your individual rate of calorie burning with Pole Walking with Metabolic Equivalent (MET).
2. Use a calorie calculator (www.mypyramid.gov).
3. Calculate your daily calorie intake to maintain your body weight after you have achieved your target weight.
4. Body-Mass-Index (BMI).

The Metabolic Equivalent (MET)

The Metabolic Equivalent (MET) is used to compare the energy consumption of different activities. It defines the metabolism of a human when resting in comparison to his body weight.

The scientific definition:
1 MET means a calorie consumption of 1 kcal per kilogram (= 2.2lb) of body weight per hour. (Ainsworth et al., 1993).

This makes it possible to calculate calorie consumption for different physical activities.

Energy consumption / Calorie burning rate with sports per hour:		
Sitting	→	1MET
Raking a lawn (1hr)	→	4MET
Walking	→	5MET (4 mph)
Nordic Pole Walking	→	7MET (5 mph)
Jogging	→	10MET (6.5 mph)

Body weight and body fat

Everybody, including the weight loss industry, is talking about losing body weight. It is more correct to talk about losing **body fat**.

When you weigh your body after physical exercise, the scale tells you that you have lost 1 pound. The truth is that you lose approx. 50% water and 50% body fat. Due to your individual body composition and your metabolism, the rate might be 60:40. Scientists call this the "**Relative fat burning rate.**"

The 50 percent of water you lose is replaced quickly because you eat and drink after your workout. If you avoid eating sugar and fat, the burned 50 percent of body fat is gone forever.

There is another point you should know: when you train your muscles they get stronger. Muscles are five times as dense as fat. Therefore, your body gets shaped and slim in time, but you have to consider the weight of your stronger muscles when stepping on your scale. However, you realize that your clothes fit much better.

A simple self-test: Stand in front of a mirror, lift your arms and watch yourself. Do you like what you see?

Pole Walking and weight management make your body fat melt away.

In addition to your scale, take a tape-measure to measure your hip and abdomen. You will realize that you can go back to a smaller dress size.

Now you know that you have to lose body fat to lose real weight.

As a well-educated Pole Walker from now on, you will define your target weight loss as a loss of body fat.

Example: If somebody tells you he/she wants to lose four pounds of body weight, you know that means two pounds of body fat (approximately 50 percent).
This is real weight loss.

Consider:
"Body-fat-loss" averages 50 % of the general term "body-weight-loss"

The Tape Measure tells more than a scale …

Body Mass Index: lower than 20

Calculate your Body Mass Index (BMI)

Classification of BMI			
BMI Classification	**Category**	**Men**	**Women**
Underweight	0	< 20	< 19
Normal Weight	1	20-24.9	19-23.9
Overweight	2	25-29.9	24-29.9
Obese	3	30-39.9	30-39.9
Massivly Obese	4	> 40	> 40

On many websites you will find an automatic calculation BMI. Just fill in your body weight and body height (www.mypyramid.gov).

The formula for the U.S.:

$$BMI = (703 \times Body\ Weight\ (LB)) : (Height\ (in) \times Height\ (in))$$

The BMI corresponds with age:

Years of Age	BMI
19-24	19-24
25-34	20-25
35-44	21-26
45-54	22-27
55-64	23-28
Over 64	24-29

Source: DGE

If your BMI is more than 25, start thinking about losing weight.

To learn more about parameters like "Compare your Body Weight" and "Hip-to-Waist Ratio" go to chapter 15 "A Great Tool to Change Your Lifestyle."

Do not starve yourself to keep your target body weight stable

If the caloric intake needed to keep your body weight down is too small ("starving"), your body does not get the nutrition it needs to function well and be healthy.

With a diet like this, you not only lose body fat (which is the primary goal), but you lose muscle mass and you can damage your cells. Even with a therapeutic fast you need to eat "high volume" foods to guarantee sufficient nutrition of your cells (see chapter 7.1: "Berlin Weight Loss Concept"). For a short period (three to seven days), you can fast – as recommended in the following chapter – first to get water out of your body and enhance detoxification. Then cut out sugar and eat the right fat – and exercise to continue burning your body fat.

To stay energized, to keep your organs and your brain in good health, and maintain your successfully achieved target weight, you need a daily calorie intake according to your individual normal body weight (BMI 20-24.9).

Use the following formula when you have achieved your target weight to help you maintain it:

Normal Body Weight x 24 Hours.

Example for a normal body weight woman:

Body weight: 143 lb

$$\frac{143\,(lb) \times 24\,(hours)}{2.2} = 1{,}560 \text{ kcal}$$

The daily caloric intake should be 1,560kcal of "high-volume" foods.

Man: Body weight: 184 lb

$$\frac{184\,(lb) \times 24\,(hours)}{2.2} = 2{,}016 \text{ kcal}$$

The caloric intake per day should be 2,016 kcal of "high-volume" foods.

It is surprising how consciously walkers chose foods when starting to control the amount of calories they eat and drink. A good source to check calorie content of foods is www.MyPyramid.gov.

Weight loss with Nordic Pole Walking

I will present two scientific studies about weight loss with Nordic Pole Walking. Study 1 describes how effective Walking works in combination with a diet program. With study 2, you can determine your target fat loss and amount of walking miles you will need.

Study 1: Pure diet against diet & Walking

This German study compared 136 participants to find out what is more effective, to lose weight or to lower the BMI index.

One group started a diet without walking exercise. The second group started a combination of diet and walking program. The age differed from 18 – 65. The Body Mass Index differed from 29.3 – 31.6 (overweight to obese).

The results prove that the combination of good nutrition and walking exercise is a successful "therapy." This group lost nearly 5 pounds more in the same amount of time. (Source: Mommert-Jauch, 2003).

The Result:
The group with the diet and walking program lowered their BMI an average of 7.3 % which equals 6.2 Kg (= 13.64 pounds).
The group with diet only lowered the BMI an average of 4.3 %, which equals 4.4 Kg (= 8.8 pounds).

Study 2: Burning body fat & amount of Walking miles

Another German scientific study proved that Nordic Pole Walking shows positive effects for weight loss. As we learned, we have to consider body fat as a parameter for substantial weight loss. The study wanted to find out how many hours a Pole Walker has to walk to lose 1 kg (=2.2 pounds) of body fat without changing eating habits. 1 kg (=2.2 pounds) of body fat equals the energy of 7,500 kcal.

Training time and target fat loss

A simple formula calculates how many miles or time a participant needs to walk to achieve his/her target body-fat-loss with Nordic Pole Walking only. The participants were advised to not change their eating habits or reduce calorie intake during the study.

This Pole Walker weighs 198 lbs and wants to lose 2.2 lbs of body fat.	
Body weight:	198 lbs
Target Body Fat Loss:	2.2 lbs
Fat Burning Rate:	25 % (Due to his body structure he had a fat burning rate of 25:75;= 25% fat and 75% water)
Training session:	1 hour each session
Nordic Pole Walking:	7 MET

The Formula:

$$\text{Kcal/hr} = (\text{MET} \times \text{Body Weight (lb)}) : (\text{Target Fat Loss (lb)})$$

1. Put in the data from above:

Kcal/hr = (7 MET x 198 lb (Body Weight)) : 2.2lb (Target Fat Loss)
Kcal/hr = 1,386 : 2.2
Kcal/hr = 630
Fat Burning Rate 25% = 157.5 kcal/hr.

That means this man burns 472.5 kcal/hr body fat when Pole Walking 3 miles per hour.

Remember the target fat loss is 1 kg (2.2 lbs) which equals the energy of 7,500 kcal.

2. How many hours does it take this man to walk to burn these 7,500 kcal?

It's easy to calculate:

Divide 7,500 kcal by 472.5 kcal fat burning rate per hour (3 miles).

Target Fat Loss = 7,500 kcal divided by 472.5 kcal/hr = 15.9

Hours to pole walk: 15.9 = 16 hrs.

To burn 2.2 pounds of pure body fat, the man needs to pole walk 16 hours.

3. He wants to achieve his target weight loss in 2 months (8 weeks):

Total training 16 hours

Goal: 8 weeks

16 hours : 8 weeks = 2 hrs/week

Result:
To lose 2.2 pounds of body fat after 8 weeks he has to pole walk 2 hours per week.

Now fill your bodyweight and target FAT-loss into the formula to find out how many hours you have to pole walk to achieve your fat loss target and to calculate how many weeks it will take to achieve your goal. This will depend on how often you want to pole walk per week.

Calculate your amount of walking time to lose your target fat loss:

- your body weight
- your target body fat loss

MET for Nordic Pole Walking: 7

Kcal/hr = (7 (MET) x Your body weight) : (Your target fat loss)

Amount of kcal of your target fat loss:	
Energy of lb(kg) Body Fat	Kcal
Energy of 1.1 lb (0.5kg) of body fat	3,750
Energy of 2.2 lb (1.0kg) of body fat	7,500
Energy of 3.6 lb (1.5kg) of body fat	11,250
Energy of 4.4 lb (2.0kg) of body fat	15,000

Sources for weight loss concepts

"Make the right choice of food and calories to reach your sustainable target weight while staying healthy and enjoying eating."

Find the right balance between your physical activities, your caloric intake and your choice of enjoyable foods. Making the right food choices from the broad range of healthy food available is not difficult.

The following chapter will help you.

This book offers two proven sources to:

- make smart choices from every food group
- find your balance between food and physical activity
- get the most nutrition out of your calorie-intake
- stay within your daily caloric needs

Source number one:

The United States Department of Agriculture (USDA) provides a wonderful, practical, interactive web site, which helps you learn a lot about foods, calories, and menus. This will assist you in making the right choices for enjoyable and healthy eating:

www.MyPyramid.gov
United States Department of Agriculture

"MyPyramid Tracker" offers a detailed assessment of your food intake and physical activity level.

Source number two:

The Berlin Weight Loss Concept that we practiced in Germany with our patients was very successful for years. This German concept, as described in the next chapter, goes along with the information at "MyPyramid.gov". Also of note is the innovative book "The Better Brain Book" by David Perlmutter, a leader in the field of complementary medicine from Naples, Florida.

These sources give you all the information you need and will help you on your way to a better life!

Two goals you will achieve:

Happy with your scale and happy in life

7.1   The BERLIN-Weight Loss Concept

This easy-to-understand concept helps you to:

- Lose weight

- Learn to eat right ("high-volume" food)

- Maintain your target weight for the rest of your life

Before reading on, I would like to explain the benefits of this concept.

In Berlin, Germany, we have practiced this concept very successfully in our medical office for years. All participants achieved their target weights and most of them have been successful in maintaining it. Even participants who returned to their former eating habits, started all over again and have been successful since.

The first three weeks are key to long-term success.

The 3 Golden Rules:

- Drink instead of eating

- Avoid sugar

- Consume less fat

Within the first three weeks you lose between 5-10 lbs in a healthy and sustainable way.

First three days
You begin with a 3 day therapeutic "fast" that includes 4 "high-volume" meals. The purpose of the first 3 days is weight loss, washing water out of your body, detoxifying and experiencing immediate success.

First three weeks
The purpose of the following weeks is to lose body fat when you eat 'high-volume' foods. There are many recipe-books on the market (see David Perlmutter 2004). It gives your body the time to change its metabolism – the basis to keep your weight low.

Drink a lot
Learn to drink 2 to 3 liters a day. Drink chemical-free mineral water and fresh made fruit juice, tea, plus low sugar (5g/100 ml) isotonic drinks.

The best drinks to insure plenty of minerals are a mixture of fruit & vegetable juices and mineral water.

Most people drink too little and suffer from latent dehydration. Your liquid intake should be a minimum of 2-3 liters per day. That eliminates your hunger as well. Drink, even though you do not feel "really" thirsty, to make sure your body gets sufficient liquids.

Avoid soft drinks. Even canned juices often contain a huge amount of artificial sugar. A high sugar diet can result in damaging cells and cause more body fat.

Dehydration

Dehydration begins with a loss of liquid of 2 to 4 percent of body weight – that's about 0.6 to 1.6 liters. More than 5 percent of a decreased liquid level can cause dizziness and bloodflow disturbances. Before exercising, you should drink about 400 to 600 ml and have your drink-bottle with you to drink in between your exercise.

Avoid dehydration

Before Walking	During Walking	After Walking
Start fluid intake in the mornings	When more than 1 hour	Additional 1-2 liters up to a daily intake of 2- 3 liters
Medium temperature	150-200 ml each 15-10 Minutes	
200 ml 15 Min. before training	Drink slowly	
1:3 Mix of Juice:Water	1:5 Mix of Juice:Water	1:1 Mix of Juice:Water

(Source: A. Schroff)

Avoid low-value carbohydrates

We have learned to eat less fat, but instead are consuming more carbohydrates. In the Western hemisphere, and especially in the U.S., people continue to gain weight because the "wrong" carbohydrates are consumed.

Often, we eat sweets not because we are hungry, but because we need some 'oral satisfaction.'

Avoid cookies, chocolate, cake, white bread, etc. that contain the so-called "bad" low-value carbohydrates. These carbohydrates have no "high-volume" value. Eating these leads to high insulin levels. Insulin restricts fat-burning!

The more you force your body to produce insulin by eating "bad" carbohydrates, the less fat you burn. Additionally, these low-value carbohydrates are stored as "new" fat in your body. When eating sweets, your insulin "jumps" to a very high level and then drops to a very low level, which results in a feeling of hunger. You start eating again - a true deadend-circle.

Eat good carbohydrates

By understanding these simple facts, switch to the "high-volume" carbohydrates like fruits and whole grain bread. Good carbohydrates do not raise your insulin to a level that restricts fat burning.

What about eating fat?

Our body needs fat! Our brain especially needs fat, because it is the most metabolically active organ in the body. The brain needs fat more than any other organ, because it uses fat as fuel.

The daily intake of fat for a normal weight person should be:
1g fat per kg Normal Body Weight.

Example: 1g fat X 65 kg = 65 g fat per day

The four primary categories of fat we eat:

- Monounsaturated fat
- Saturated fat
- Polyunsaturated fat
- Trans-fatty acids

Monounsaturated fat
This is a cell and brain-friendly fat. It is found in common cooking oils, like olive oil, canola oil and some forms of safflower oil, nuts, and avocados. These fats contain high antioxidants and are subject to less oxidative damage than other types of fat.

Saturated fat

It is a low energy fat. Saturated fat is found primarily in animal origin food, like beef, lamb, pork, chicken, eggs and whole-fat dairy products. These fats are more prone to oxidative damage than monounsaturated fat, which can increase the risk of free radical damage to your cells.

Ten percent of saturated fat in your daily caloric intake is fine, but most Americans eat three times more than is necessary every day. Eating diets high in saturated fat can raise the level of homocysteine, the amino acid that can cause memory problems and increases the risk of Alzheimer's disease.

Polyunsaturated fat

We need to get polyunsaturated fat from our food, because it includes all-important essential fatty acids and cannot be produced by our body.

The two types of essential fatty acids are:

- Omega-3 fatty acids
- Omega-6 fatty acids

Omega 3 fatty acids are found in cold water fatty fish, dark green vegetables and some grains and seeds. Many people do not take in enough omega-3 fatty acids, which split into eicosapentanoic (EPA) and docosahexaenoic acid (DHA). A low level of DHA can cause a decrease of cognitive function, depression, moodiness, slow response time, irritability and Alzheimer's disease.

Avoid trans-fatty acids

Trans-fats are synthetic fats that are primarily found in processed baked food, fried foods, and in most margarines. These trans-fatty acids destroy the cell's ability to make energy, get adequate nutrition, or to communicate with other cells. Trans-fats are also linked to an increased risk of diabetes and heart disease.

Conclusion

Cut out trans-fatty acids.

You find this in foods like commercial bread, crackers, frozen waffles, cookies and snack food.

Bake, sauté, steam or grill when you cook. Any fat heated to a high temperature will result in trans-fatty acids. Avoid French fries, donuts, and most types of chips. Read the labels before buying food.

Reduce your intake of saturated fat.
Meat and full-fat dairy products are the major sources of saturated fat Americans eat. Look for the leanest cuts of beef.

Increase your intake of Omega 3 fatty acids.
Fish, fresh greens, walnuts, pumpkin seeds and eggs are great sources of omega 3 fatty acids.

Protein

Protein is essential for cell repair and the maintenance of our body.

The daily protein intake should be:

0.8 g protein per 2.2 lb body weight

Example: 0.8 g of protein X 143 lb body weight = 52 g protein per day.

Most of the protein we eat is from meat. Another good choice is to eat protein from plant sources, like tofu (bean curd) and tempeh (fermented soybean patty). Soy-based foods are low in saturated fat and a good alternative to meat. They contain antioxidants and protect against free radicals. (Source: D. Perlmutter 2004).

If you have a deeper interest in learning how food influences your body positively or negatively and would like to have some great cooking recipes, I recommend "The Better Brain Book", a cutting-edge book, written by David Perlmutter. In our medical office in Germany, we incorporate Perlmutter's advice into our nutritional counseling with great success.

How Acupuncture can help

In our medical practice, acupuncture is a supportive therapy. Participants receive three very tiny permanent acupuncture needles into three relevant points on the ear:

- the anti-addiction point
- the anti-aggression point
- the anti-depression point.

Wearing these permanent needles for three weeks helps to change your eating behaviors. It also suppresses eagerness, controls appetite and keeps you in a positive mood.

The Nordic Pole Walking program works without acupuncture as well. However, we recommend acupuncture because it helps without having side effects.

Now get started with your BERLIN Weight Loss Concept

7.2 Body Change in 3 Weeks

The BERLIN weight loss concept

Program:

- Personal food check: Analyze your daily food intake for "high-fat/high sugar" quality.

- Measure your body fat on day "one".

- Three days of therapeutic fast .

- Reduced "high fat/high sugar" food.

- Weight control with the help of 'fasting-days'.

- Conscious nutrition is your target.

- Re-measure your body fat after 21 days.

- Acupuncture to support body change.

7.3 The 3 Golden Rules

1. Drinking instead of eating

2. Avoid fat

3. Avoid sugar

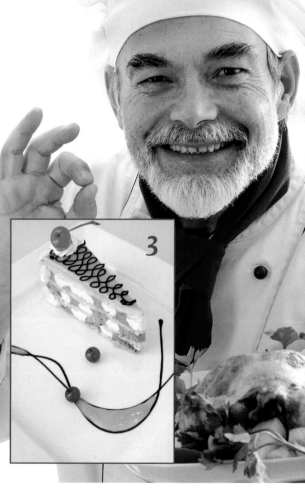

7.4 Reduced Calorie Nutritional Food

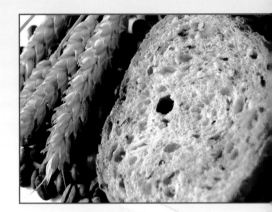

- **2 slices crispbread + farmers or low-fat cottage cheese with herbs, tea (honey) or**

- **1 slice whole grain bread + farmers or low-fat cottage cheese, tea (honey)**

- **Vegetables or salad**

- **1 low-fat yogurt (1.5%) + 1 apple + tea (honey)**

- **Turkey, chicken or fish steamed with potatoes (1-2 small ones) or rice (1-2 tablespoons), plus salad**

7.5   3 Days of Therapeutic Fast

- 4 "nutritional" meals per day -

Morning:

1 banana

Black tea with honey

Noon:

1 vegetable soup or

1 salad

Afternoon:

1 yoghurt

1 apple

Tea with honey

Evening:

1 turkey breast or

1 salad

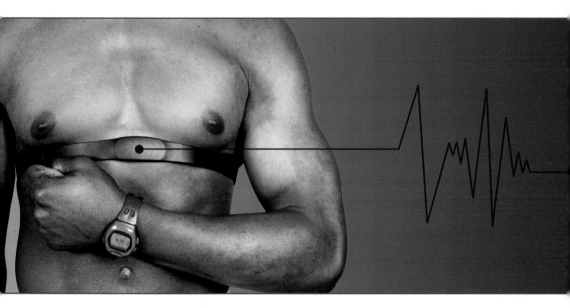

Improve Your Cardio Power

8

To benefit most from Nordic Pole Walking, first find out what your best training intensity level is. This chapter offers you a basic understanding of how to best train your cardio-system and how to find your range of training intensity.

Watch your pulse

The faster you walk the faster your heart beats. Your heart pumps more blood to provide more oxygen to your muscles. Your pulse is the parameter that tells you if you are walking at the most beneficial speed or if you should slow down.

Anaerobic Walking – Do not walk too fast in the beginning

If you walk too fast your cardio system will not be able to provide enough oxygen for your muscles. They will become "oxygen deprived." Your muscles can retrieve energy without oxygen when burning sugar (glycogen), which is stored in your muscles for a certain amount of time. Then, almost no fat is burned down. We call this the "anaerobic threshold."

97

Pace Walking

The "problem" is, you can walk at this intense pace only for a relatively short time, because the glycogen is limited. However, glycogen does not burn out completely and the rest of it stays in your muscles as lactate.

Anaerobic walking is inappropriate for health-training: if you have too much lactate in your blood, your stress-hormones increase and your immune system weakens. Also, you will feel really sore after this high-impact training session.

The conclusion: Don't walk too fast, especially as a beginner. It is not fun to be sore for two or three days and you will hurt your body more than you will profit from it.

Aerobic Walking – The healthy way

The range where your muscles are fueled with sufficient oxygen while walking is called the aerobic range.

When walking in this range, your muscles burn fat and sugar completely. Only water and CO_2 are formed. This is what you want to accomplish in order to burn down your body fat. This is the correct training intensity level you should walk with.

As you can see from the explanation of anaerobic and aerobic training range, there is a threshold at which your cardiovascular system switches from burning fat to burning sugar (glycogen) and when it begins to produce more (too much) lactate. We call this "threshold pulse."

This threshold in your blood begins when there is approximately 4 mmol/l lactate in your blood. This level starts the range for advanced fitness and athletic training. To find out at what pace your individual anaerobic threshold begins, consult a doctor of sports-medicine for a lactate-test – which is taken on the lobe of your ear while walking on a treadmill.

Avoid crossing this threshold as a beginner. "Listen to your muscles" during your first outdoor walking session as to whether or not you feel soreness. If you do, you walked too fast.

Advanced Walkers shift their anaerobic threshold higher step-by-step, but this is not crucial for health sports.

Determine your personal and optimal Walking tempo

Your pulse is an individual parameter that is influenced by age, emotions, fitness level, being male or female, health disorders, medications, etc. There are scientifically proven definitions to determine your optimal individual training pulse according to your goals:

- Walking for recreation
- Walking or fat burning
- Performance or Race Walking

You determine your individual walking goals by the percentage of heartbeats of your maximum heartbeat frequency (HFmax).

To determine your maximum heartbeat frequency without being tested on a treadmill, use the definition used in sports medicine all around the world:

Maximum heartbeat frequency (HFmax):

Men: 220 minus age
Women: 226 minus age

Example:
220 minus 49 = 171 HFmax (men)
220 minus 49 = 177 HFmax (women)

There are three pulse ranges defined for Walking:

Recreation: 55% - 65% of HFmax
Fat Burning: 65% - 75% of HFmax
Performance/Racing: 75% - 85% of HFmax

Walking exercise below 55% of HFmax is just like walking the dog. It is good to move, but you have no training effect on your cardiovascular system when you do it for less than 1 hour. When walking at this tempo for more than 1 hour, it will show positive health effects on your cardiovascular system, but at a lower level.

To determine your personal training pulse according to your training goals, use the following formula for each training range:

Recreation Walking: 55% - 65% of HFmax

Men: (220 – age) x .55 - .65
Women:(226 – age) x .55 - .65

Example:
Men: 220 – 49 = 171 x .65 = 111 bts/min
Women: 226 – 49 = 177 x .65 = 115 bts/min

Fat burning zone: 65% - 75% of HFmax

Men: (220 – age) x .65 - .75
Women: (226 – age) x .65 - .75

Example:
Men: (220 – 49) = 171 x .75 = 128 bts/min
Women: (226 – 49) = 177 x .75 = 132 bts/min

Performance Walking: 75% - 85% of HFmax

Men: (220 – age) x .75 - .85
Women: (226 – age) x .75 - .85

Example:
Men: (220 – 49) = 171 x .85 = 145 bts/min
Women: (226 – 49) = 177 x .85 = 150 bts/min

The "fat burning zone"

To burn most of your body fat, the best walking pace is at plus/ minus 130 bts/min as a rule of thumb.

The good news is: You often hear that body fat burning begins after 30 minutes of walking. That's correct when you are a beginner.

After 3 months of Pole Walking, your muscles have "learned" to burn fat right from the first minute.

Consider: The faster you walk, the more sugar (glycogen) and less fat you burn. If you walk with less than 65% of HFmax, you will not burn much body fat, or you will have to walk longer (one to two hours), which is good training for the fat burning metabolism.

As an improved walker, when taking a shorter walk of only 30 minutes, you should walk a bit faster (65 – 85% of HFmax), as long as you feel well and comfortable with this tempo.

Weight loss combined with walking exercise improves your cardio System the most.

Each lost kilogram (2.2 lbs) of body weight decreases your blood pressure about 1.7 mmHg, and if your BMI is over 25, it is appropriate to combine good 'high-volume' nutrition with (Pole) Walking (See chapter 7 "Weight Loss with Nordic Pole Walking").

Be smart, and consider your health improvement as a holistic approach (See chapter 15 "A Great Tool to Change Your Lifestyle").

Training principles for beginners

Start slowly!
If you have not exercised regularly for years, for the first 4 weeks walk in the Recreation and Fat Burning Zone. Listen to your body.

With Pole Walking your muscles get stronger and the tendons, joints and bones increase stability. It takes some time. Your muscles adapt five times faster than your tendons and cartilage. If you feel some soreness in your tendons and joints, take a break for a few days.

Distance comes before speed!
As soon as you feel ready for more miles, increase your walking distance and keep your pulse rate (speed) at this level. This way, your body has a chance to adapt your cardiovascular system, metabolism, joints and tendons.

Control your pulse!

Manual pulse control

To control the walking speed that helps you achieve your goals, it is necessary to check your heartbeats per minute while walking. It is easy to do:

All you need is a wrist watch that shows seconds. Feel your pulse either at your wrist on the side where your thumb is or at your aorta in your neck.

Count your pulse for 10 seconds and multiply by 6. Now you have your heartbeats per minute. It's only a slight inconvenience to stop and take your pulse.

Interrupting your walk may lower your pulse by 10 to 20 beats. This method is not exact, but it gives you a pulse range at which you are walking.

Heart rate/calorie monitor

A heart rate monitor is a better choice. You don't have to stop to see your actual pulse as displayed of your wrist monitor.

To obtain the most accurate data, choose a model that has a chest-strap, which measures the heartbeats right at your heart. These impulses are transferred to your wrist-watch and are quite accurate. A popular manufacturer is POLAR.

Shows pulse & kcal.

You can purchase models which also display the amount of calories you burn. You can also preset the pulse rate range in which you want to train. Pulse rate monitors are available in sporting goods stores starting at $70.00.

Pedometer

Pedometers count the number of steps you walk.
A rule of thumb for a healthy lifestyle is 10,000 steps per day.
Look for a pedometer that automatically converts your steps into calories burned. Pedometers are not as accurate as heart rate monitors, but will provide you with the basic data for your training program.

How often should you walk per week?

Scientific studies have proven that:

Burning 1,500 to 2,000 calories per week in addition to your daily life activities protects against many diseases. To protect yourself, just adhere to what you have learned in earlier explanations. In summary, Pole Walking for three hours a week will lead to better health.

It does not matter if you pole-walk three days for one hour or six days for thirty minutes each day. This is the range in which you should train to improve your health significantly. There is no reason for additional training, unless you are training for "competition" (races).

In chapter 17 "Plans for Your Success" you will find training plans for each fitness level to achieve your personal goals.

Check the "Fitness Calculator" to find the training schedule that fits your personal goals. Your may be a "Beginner", an "Improved Walker", an "Advanced Walker", or a "Performance Walker" who is preparing for NPW-10K, NPW- Half-Marathon or NPW-Marathon walks.

Prevent or Fight Diabetes

9

We decided to include this chapter because diabetes is growing so rapidly. The World Health Organization predicts that the number of people who suffer from diabetes will double within the next 13 years!

Diabetes risk factors

- High blood pressure

- Obesity

- Disturbances of fat-metabolism

- High blood sugar

This epidemic of the 21st century is called the "Deadly Quartet" or scientific-ally spoken, the "Metabolic Syndrome."

Reasons for this pessimistic perspective are: Incorrect nutritional behavior and reduced physical activity.

With little exercise, your metabolism reacts slowly and does not tolerate insulin well. Consequently, insulin-resistance develops and leads to Type 2 Diabetes. In addition, we are dealing with a large group of people who have genetic diabetes. Check with your parents and grandparents as to whether there is diabetes in your family. There might be a high probability that you will develop diabetes at some point in your life. If so, start doing regular physical activity right now.

Since diabetes is often accompanied by high blood pressure, obesity and disturbances of the fat-metabolism, the probability for developing arteriosclerosis, heart attack, brain stroke, diabetes foot (less blood flow in the feet), diabetic retinopathy, diabetic nephropathy and diabetic poly-neuropathy is increased.

How to lower your risk:

Studies show that the risk of suffering from diabetes can be reduced by burning extra calories through exercising:

- 500 kcal per week can lower the risk by 6%.

- 2.5 hours of walking per week can lower the risk by 45%.

- 3.5 hours of walking per week can lower the risk by 65%.

Regular physical activities lower your blood sugar, blood fat, blood pressure and improve insulin resistance. It also cures existing diabetes to a certain level. Often medication can be reduced.

You can define your personal risk for diabetes according to the following risk parameters (valid for the Western hemisphere):

Besides the risk-factor from unhealthy abdominal size, two more of the following health-disorders must be present.

Check your personal risk for diabetes:

Risk Factor	Parameters
Unhealthy Abdominal Circumference (Abdominal Distention)	MEN: more than 94 cm
	WOMEN: more than 80 cm
2 or more Health Disorders:	
Triglycerides	More than 150 mg/dl
HDL-Cholesterol	MEN: under 40 mg/dl WOMEN: under 50 mg/dl
Blood Pressure	More than 130/85 mmHg
Blood Sugar (fasting)	More than 110 mg/dl for Type 2 Diabetes

(Mommert-Jauch 2004)

If your abdominal circumference is more than 94 cm (for men) or 80 cm (for women) and you have two or more of the above health disorders, you should consult your health professional.

Check your blood sugar status

Good	At risk	Needs therapy

Glucose (before breakfast) mg/dl – mmol/l

3.0	4.5	5.6	6.2	6.8	7.8	5.6

60	70	80	90	100	110	120	130	140	150
									and more

(S. Schwanbeck, 2002)

New quality of life for diabetics

The good news:
A German scientific study proved the benefits of Nordic Pole Walking with 19 patients who suffered from diabetes.

After three months of Nordic Pole Walking for 90 minutes per week,

- Patients reduced their body weight by 1.5 kg = 3.3 pounds.

- Some patients did not need anti-Diabetes medication on the day they did Pole Walking, or were able to reduce their doses.

- Furthermore, the HbA1c improved by 1.5%. HbA1c is a form of hemoglobin that glucose connects to. This parameter is used continuously to monitor the blood sugar level in Diabetes patients.

They gained more in quality of life, reduced their expenses for medication, increased their self-esteem, and connected to new friends. This is great news for everybody who suffers from diabetes!

Nordic Pole Walking is the ideal sports activity for diabetics

We know that legions of people start exercising but quit, either because the exercise they tried was too exhausting for them – like jogging – or it hurt their joints, etc. Also joining a fitness center did not result in a long-term commitment.

In Europe, millions of people who had quit other exercise sports, embraced Walking and Nordic Pole Walking instead.

Criteria for an ideal sport:

Appropriate for all ages:

- No risk
- Easy technique
- Adaptive intensity
- No great impact on joints
- Can perform everywhere
- Able to do year-round
- Not expensive

Nordic Pole Walking has it all!

What a diabetic should know before starting training:

Talk to your health care provider

If you have diabetes you should consult your doctor to discuss the adjustment of medication and nutrition for your training.

Exercise and insulin

Of course, Nordic Pole Walking consumes energy like any other sports activity. Type 2 Diabetics, who take diabetes pills or insulin, need to incorporate some therapy adjustments. Before doing a longer exercise, insulin injections and oral doses have to be reduced or the intake of nutrition has to be increased: For example 10 grams of carbohydrates per 30 minutes of exercise.

When a diabetic has taken an insulin injection, a certain level of insulin is already in the body. In conjunction with exercising longer, hypoglycemia (low blood sugar) could develop, because the insulin can decrease the release of sugar and fat, which are needed for muscle activity. Energy for muscle activity is derived from blood sugar.

When the blood sugar level is high, muscle activity usually normalizes the blood sugar level. When the blood sugar level is normal to low before exercising, this could result in hypoglycemia. For Type 2 Diabetics, this doesn't happen often. Normally, we have a combination of high blood sugar level and insulin-resistance.

Low impact exercising like Pole Walking is the ideal therapy for diabetics.

Always measure blood sugar before, during and after your exercise.

If your blood sugar level before exercising is 5-6 mmol/l, you have to eat an additional 10-15 grams of carbohydrates. If your blood sugar level is about 15 mmol/l too high, you should not exercise!

Lower amounts of insulin due to exercise saves on insulin costs.

As we learned before, your body continues to be efficient with blood sugar after exercising. You need less insulin after exercise training.

Avoid hypoglycemia

Symptoms of hypoglycemia (low blood sugar) are realized the same way when exercising. If it happens, you should immediately take 10-12 grams of fast working carbohydrates like hard candies, fruit juice or fruits.

You should always have hard candies with you when exercising. However, it's best to start your exercise program well-prepared.

Nutrition & fitness

There is no specific diabetes food. For diabetics, the general recommendations for healthy nutrition are valid:

Eat balanced low-fat food with abundant carbohydrates and roughage.

Balanced nutrition is key for diabetics: Carbohydrates increase the blood sugar level; fat and protein in normal doses do not.

It is wrong for diabetics to avoid carbohydrates and eat more fat and protein which results in weight gain with negative consequences for the metabolism.

The best composition of a good nutrition is as follows:

- Carbohydrates

- Fat

- Protein

General recommendations are that nutritional food should contain:

- 50-55 % carbohydrates

- 30-35 % fat

- 15-20 % protein

Conclusion

Low impact endurance training like Walking and Pole Walking, especially for overweight people with Type 2 Diabetes, is highly recommended.

Besides lowering blood sugar, it improves cardiovascular risk-factors like obesity, high blood fat and high blood pressure.

Fun, Friends & Fitness

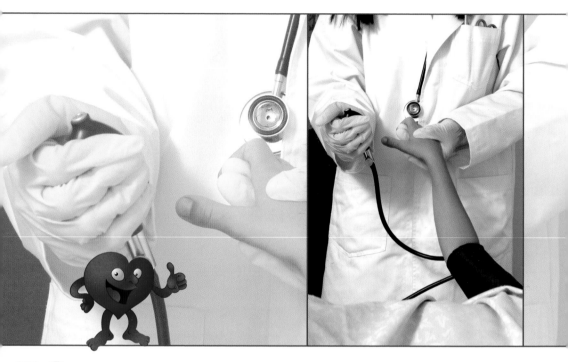

IO Prevent & Fight High Blood Pressure

High blood pressure means the pressure in your arteries is elevated. Blood pressure is the force of blood pushing against the blood vessel walls. It's written as two numbers: for example 112/78 mmHg. The top, or first number, is the systolic number and references the pressure when the heart beats. The bottom or second number is the diastolic number and represents the pressure when the heart rests between beats.

Normal blood pressure is below 120/80 mm Hg. If you are an adult and your systolic pressure is above 120 to 139, or your diastolic pressure is 80 to 89 (or both), then you have "pre-hypertension". High blood pressure is a pressure of 140 systolic or higher and /or 90 diastolic or higher that stays high over time.

There are many reasons for high blood pressure. High blood pressure has no symptoms. It's truly a "silent killer" (according to the American Heart Association). Often, it's caused by stress, which increases stress hormones like Adrenalin, Noradrenalin and Cortisol.

Check your high blood pressure risk

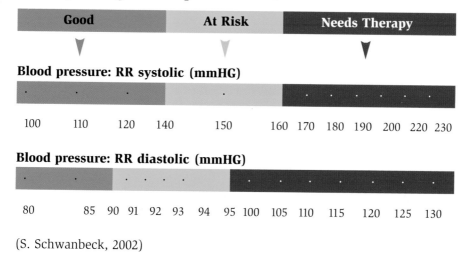

| Good | At Risk | Needs Therapy |

Blood pressure: RR systolic (mmHG)

100   110   120   140   150   160   170   180   190   200   220   230

Blood pressure: RR diastolic (mmHG)

80   85   90   91   92   93   94   95   100   105   110   115   120   125   130

(S. Schwanbeck, 2002)

What you can do

Have your blood pressure checked as soon as possible. Patients who are diagnosed with high blood pressure and take medication to lower it, should inform their Pole Walking Instructor. Well-educated instructors will always ask if their walkers take high blood pressure medication.

A beta-blocker can reduce heartbeats by 30 beats per minute. Your instructor needs to be aware that you take a beta-blocker to lower your blood pressure while participating in a Walking Program, so that you can control the intensity of your pulse rate.

He or she should know that your blood pressure is lower because of this medication.

The good news

Scientific studies show that a moderate walk twice a week for 30 to 40 minutes lowers blood pressure and the rate of heartbeats per minute.

The more you walk, the more your cardiovascular system adapts to this physical activity. Your blood pressure decreases and there are fewer heartbeats per minute. Altogether, your cardiovascular system is working much more efficiently. You won't get out of breath anymore when climbing stairs and your recovery time is much shorter after any exercise.

How Nordic Pole Walking lowers high blood pressure

Characteristics			Systolic (mmHg)	Diastolic (mmHg)
BMI		< 24.5	-3.9	-2.4
		24.5 – 26.4	-4.5	-3.6
		> 26.4	-2.2	-1.8
Pole Walking		< 120 Min/W.	-2.8	-2.2
Training		120-150 Min/W.	-4.7	-2.1
Min/Week		> 150 Min/W.	-5.1	-2.8

Lowering (systolic) blood pressure through aerobic physical activity after four and after eight weeks

Aerobic training (50% VO2 max, equals a moderate walking pace), twice a week for 30-40 minutes plus 10 to 20 minutes of additional strength training, shows astonishing results for lowering systolic blood pressure.

Nordic Pole Walking, as a full-body workout (see chapter 5 "Total Body workout"), can accomplish this for you.

Training your cardiovascular system doesn't have an "isolated" effect on your body – it's a "holistic" approach to better health and performance. In addition to exercising, we strongly recommend that you consider the quality of your nutrition as well (see chapter 7 "Weight Loss with Nordic Pole Walking").

Each Kilogram (= 2.2 lbs) of weight-loss lowers systolic blood pressure (first or top number) by 2.5 mmHg, and lowers the diastolic pressure (second or bottom number) by about 1.7 mmHg.

Your blood-fat level decreases and your metabolism begins working more efficiently. Your body-fat reduces and you decrease your risk of diabetes, stroke and heart attack. and best of all:

Your total well-being improves and you enjoy a more active lifestyle!

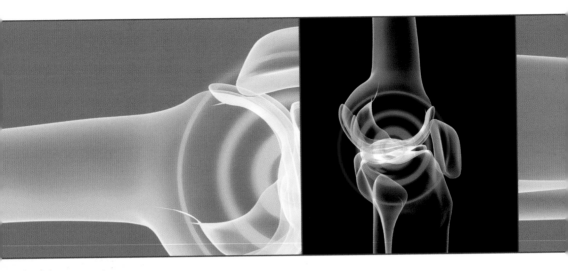

11 Prevent & Fight Arthritis

Some of our Nordic Pole Walking group members suffer from arthritis. They all agree they feel more comfortable walking with the Poles than without them.

Arthritis is the biggest enemy of our joints.

Arthritis is the number one cause of chronic disability in the United States. Affecting nearly 40 million Americans, it refers to more than 100 diseases that cause pain, stiffness and swelling from inflammation of a joint or the area around joints.

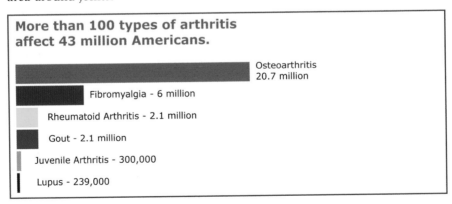

More than 100 types of arthritis affect 43 million Americans.

Osteoarthritis 20.7 million

Fibromyalgia - 6 million

Rheumatoid Arthritis - 2.1 million

Gout - 2.1 million

Juvenile Arthritis - 300,000

Lupus - 239,000

Minnesota Department of Health

There are two basic types of arthritis:

1. Osteoarthritis

This is the most common type of arthritis, suffered by 20 million Americans, usually from middle-age to older people. The symptoms worsen over time but do not cause swelling in the joints and are not inflammatory. The cartilage that cushions the bones of the hips begins to erode, eventually allowing the bones of the joints to grind or rub

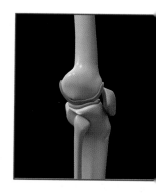

2. Rheumatoid arthritis

This is the most common type of inflammatory arthritis suffered by 2 million Americans. 75 percent are women between 30 and 60 years old, but it can develop at any age.

The inflammatory condition causes swelling in which the immune system mistakenly attacks the tissue that lines and cushions the joint.

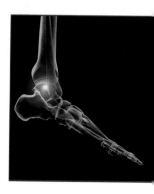

The cartilage wears away and the lining synorium becomes inflamed (swollen). The inflammation causes chemicals to be released that damage the cartilage and bone of the affected joint.

Nordic Pole Walking is a very good choice for exercise while suffering from arthritis.

Exercise your Shoulder Rotator

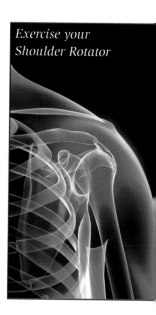

Nordic Poles stabilize your body posture and lessen the impact on hip, knee, and foot joints.

Nordic Pole Walking also exercises your hands and fingers when you swing your poles, and when you open and close your hands with each arm swing, as explained in chapter 4 "The Nordic Pole Walking Technique."

Exercising your shoulder joints helps to loosen your shoulder rotators; and with Pole Walking, you strengthen your shoulder-muscles as well.

And let's not forget about your feet and ankles: Arthritis in feet and ankle-joints is an often unseen disease. Walking and Nordic Pole Walking keep you moving and help supply blood to these locations far from your heart.

These are some reasons why many walkers who suffer from arthritis enjoy the walking exercise with Nordic poles and learn to walk distances they thought they could never walk again.

Keep walking – don't rest! You can walk more than you think ...

Reduce impact on hip, knee, and ankle joints

Stay Active!

Osteoporosis

12

Osteoporosis is a disease in which bones become fragile and are more likely to break. If not prevented – by strengthening your muscles and good nutrition – or left untreated, osteoporosis can progress painlessly until a bone breaks. These incidences, also known as fractures, occur typically in the hip, spine, and wrist. By the time a person who has osteoporosis has decreased in body height, the damage is already done.

Any bone can be affected, but of special concern are fractures of the hip and spine.

Osteoporosis is a major public health threat for an estimated 44 million Americans, or 55 percent of all people over 50 years of age.

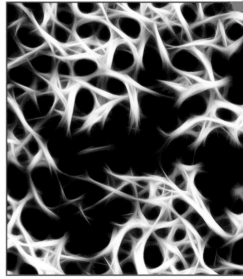

Decreased bone density

In the U.S., 10 million individuals are estimated to have this disease and almost 34 million more are estimated to have a low bone mass, placing them at increased risk for osteoporosis.

Out of the 10 million Americans estimated to have osteoporosis, eight million are women and two million are men.

Significant risk has been reported in people of all ethnic backgrounds. While osteoporosis is often thought as an older person's disease, it can strike at any age (National Osteoporosis Foundation, NOF).

What causes osteoporosis?

Both men and women achieve their "peak bone mass" between 30 and 40 years of age. From there, bone-mass gradually decreases.

Women can lose up to 20 percent of their bone mass in the five to seven years following menopause. Men with low testosterone levels are at risk as well.

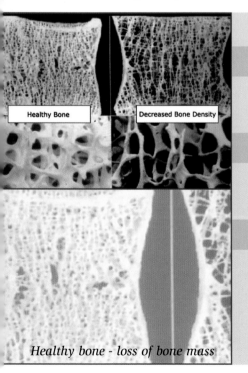

Healthy Bone

Decreased Bone Density

Healthy bone - loss of bone mass

Other risks:

- Estrogen deficiency as a result of menopause

- Abnormal absence of menstrual periods (amenorrhea)

- Low lifetime calcium intake

- Use of certain medications (corticosteroids, chemotherapy, anticonvulsants and others)

- Family history of osteoporosis

- Smoking and excessive alcohol intake

Determine your own risk

Questions	YES	NO
1 Do you have a small, thin bone frame and/or are you Caucasian or Asian?		
2 Have you or a member of your immediate family broken a bone as an adult?		
3 Have you had an early or surgically-induced menopause?		
4 Are you a menopausal woman?		
5 Have you taken high doses of thyroid medication or used glucocorticoids (for example, prednisone) for more than 3 months?		
6 Have you taken, or are you taking immunosuppressive medications or chemotherapy to treat cancer?		
7 Is your diet low in dairy products and other sources of calcium?		
8 Are you physically inactive?		
9 Do you smoke cigarettes or drink alcohol in excess?		

(Source: National Osteoporosis Foundation, USA)

The more times you answer "YES," the greater your risk for developing osteoporosis. This is the time you should talk to your health care provider.

What you can do

There are five steps to optimize bone health:

1. Muscle strengthening and resistance training.
2. A balanced diet rich in calcium and vitamin D.
3. A healthy lifestyle without smoking and excessive alcohol intake.
4. Consulting a healthcare professional about bone health.
5. Bone density testing and medication when appropriate.

Why muscle training and good nutrition is important

The good news first:

Strenuous exercise is not necessary. Easy, low-intensive activity, such as Walking and Nordic Pole Walking combined with muscle strengthening exercises (see chapter 5 "A Total Body Workout"), are most beneficial for patients with osteoporosis. Pole Walking especially trains your upright body posture.

X-rays on professional tennis players show that bone density of the typically stronger right arm, for a right-handed tennis player, is higher than the left arm. This is an easy-to-understand example of how muscle strength correlates to bone density.

When muscles gain strength, the bones have to tolerate more "force". The bones' natural reaction is to build more bone density to tolerate higher forces.

Another example are children who are raised in rural environments with a more physically active lifestyle. In comparison to children who live in inner cities with less physical activity, the rural children show a higher bone density.

If you participated in physical or sports activities in your childhood and during adolescence, your bones are generally stronger. This was an early "investment" into your bone health and you will benefit from this "health-account" for the rest of your life.

For people over 50, it is never too late to start strengthening your muscles, even if you are older than 70. If you feel you carry a risk for osteoporosis, first contact your health professional.

Nordic Pole Walking and osteoporosis

A German study on women found a significant increase in bone mass after 6 months of Pole Walking.

Because Pole Walking strengthens your leg, hip, arm and upper body muscles, it's very obvious that this is a great low-risk sports activity to prevent and to treat osteoporosis.

People who have already suffered a broken bone caused by osteoporosis, and are treated with medication, should talk to their healthcare provider before incorporating Pole Walking into their activity program.

13 Nordic Pole Walking for Healthy Veins

Your cardiovascular system is key

Your cardiovascular-system consists of your heart and blood vessels. In arteries, the oxygen-rich blood flows from your heart to your limbs, to your other organs and to your legs.

The arteries branch out to very tiny capillaries, delivering oxygen and nutrition and pick up waste and by-products. This low-oxygen blood goes from the capillaries to the veins of the legs and has to pump from there back upwards to the heart.

The vein–muscle pump

With each stride and each movement your leg muscles continuously contract and relax. In the same rhythm, the veins between your muscles squeeze and widen like a manual pump. This "mechanism" pumps your blood back to your heart.

The vein–valve

The vein-valves work only in the direction to the heart. They prevent your blood, which is pumped upwards to your heart, from flowing back.

Poor veins

With increasing age or genetic preposition, the walls of veins become slack and the veins themselves get wider.

Risk factors are:

- Long standing and sitting positions

- Lack of exercise

- Pregnancy

- Obesity

When veins grow wider, the vein-valves can't close properly anymore. The blood-flow to the heart is slower or flows backwards. This increases pressure in veins. The weakened vein walls cannot withstand this pressure and widening increases.

Because the low-oxygen blood and the by-products are not transported back fast enough, skin and tissues are insufficiently supplied with oxygen and nutrition. In addition, by-products damage cells.

By the time this overstretch of veins moves to the deeper lying veins and most of the vein-system is disturbed, chronic vein insufficiency develops.

Consequences of weak veins

- Varicosis

- Vein inflammation

- Thrombosis

- Chronic vein insufficiency

What you can do to prevent vein diseases:

The best treatments are:

- Weight loss

- Exercise

- Cold water treatment

- Medication

- Compression tapes & socks

Ask your doctor before you start exercising. You may need additional medical or physical therapy treatment.

Exercising, especially Walking and Pole Walking are the most important long-term therapies to train your muscle pumps. Lack of exercising does not activate the pump-mechanism. Regular training of your leg and foot muscles improves the function of the muscle pump and enhances blood flow in your veins.

Walking and Nordic Pole Walking are the most effective "self-medication" to prevent and help cure vein problems.

Sports activities which force high-intensity impact to your leg muscles such as tennis, soccer and basketball, are not recommended for people with vein problems. They produce a lot of residual products which then are transported improperly and increase the likelihood of damage as described above.

Stress Killer – Pole Walking and Its Influence on Mental Health

14

After a physical workout we know how good it feels to relax: Stress has gone, you feel "balanced" and your spirits are up. You experience this feeling of satisfaction because you achieved personal "success."

You cannot explain it – it has to be experienced!

Maybe you walked five miles for the first time, you enjoyed great sunny weather and a wonderful environment, or you felt that walking with your poles felt easy this day.

Medically spoken, this is caused by biochemical processes which influence your brain. Increasing your blood flow in your cardiovascular system to a certain level produces endorphins, a "feel-good hormone" influencing your mood. Active walkers know about this "great feeling" during and after walking.

Listen to your instincts. Your body is prepared to tolerate stress. The hormones adrenaline and cortisol ensured the survival of human beings for million of years. When our ancient ancestors faced a dangerous situation, adrenaline and cortisol were released instantly to set the body into "alert-status" to run away or fight quickly. Thereafter, these hormones return to normal levels through physical activity.

Nowadays, we consider adrenaline and cortisol as "negative hormones." After experiencing anger or stress, these hormones stay in your body and damage your brain, cells and metabolism. We do not "burn them down" through physical activity like our ancestors.

Today, we need to exercise to get rid of these "negative hormones."

If you overcome stressful situations or frustration with inactivity, alcohol-intake or "frustration" eating, you might suffer health disorders like psychosomatic diseases, depression and metabolic disturbances.

Scientists all around the world conducted plenty of studies on these phenomena.

Researches found that physical exercise positively influences depression, fear, negative stress, self-confidence and a general sensitivity to health disorders.

Here are some of these results:
For negative stress, especially aerobic endurance training is very effective (Alfermann and Stoll, 1997; Crews and Landers, 1987).

Arend et al. (2001) stated that physical activity has a positive influence on long-term depression and reduces manifest fear problems.

Fuchs (2003) proved that exercising has an anti-depressive effect, comparable to psycho-therapeutic treatment.

Another aspect is the long-term development of self-confidence (Woll, 2002). People performing good self confidence are psychologically more stable and suffer less psycho-somatic diseases.

Based on these studies and personal experience, more and more psychotherapists incorporate low impact exercises into their treatment concepts. Patients who started a continuous physical activity program could reduce the dosage of anti-depression medication.

Being aware of these facts, walking and Nordic Pole Walking are natural activity-concepts which help develop a higher resistance to stress, stronger self-awareness and prevent or cure psychosomatic diseases.

15 A Great Tool to Change Your Lifestyle

What does it take to change your lifestyle to be a desirable role model to your family, friends, spouse, or for business purposes?

You need to be mentally ready for this change!

The three basic components for a successful lifestyle change are:

- **Attitude**

- **Eating**

- **Activity**

If you wish to be successful, you need to make the decision to organize your daily life with some discipline and motivation to achieve your goals for mental and physical fitness.

This does not mean to live a life in "deprivation." Absolutely not!

Your new active lifestyle includes:

- Fun
- Friends
- Success in various fields
- Fitness
- Leisure time

Attitude

More than anything, your motivation is crucial for a successful lifestyle change. If you are motivated, you can achieve just about anything.

You need to recognize when you are ready and motivated for change. You will need to change some attitudes. It can make the difference between success and failure.

You can learn a lot from athletes.

Athletes learn to set goals and to have the mental strength to stay focused and motivated to achieve their goals. This does not mean they deprive themselves. They are committed to their goals.

Athletes have fun when experiencing success with every small step of improvement. It keeps their motivation high for everyday training.

They make friends as most sports require a team. That means a major part of their motivation is socialization with other people targeting the same goals.

They experience success in sports as the result of their training efforts and share it with their friends.

Many athletes are successful in business as well, because they acquired the mental ability to stay focused, disciplined and to organize their daily life. Through physical training, athletes benefit from all the health benefits we described in our earlier chapter on "Health Benefits." These help achieve the physical and mental strength and resilience to tolerate stress. However, they also enjoy leisure time. Mental and physical relaxation are both essential to be successful. Striving for success in fitness or in business without taking breaks for recreation leads to overtraining or "burn-out."

In general: A young athlete learns right from the beginning of his/her sports career to balance all elements.

Everybody, as well as yourself, can follow these principles — no matter the fitness level.

For any health-conscious person there is more involved than just setting a goal to loose weight over a three-month diet.

Why do so many people quit before achieving their goals? Because they do not incorporate a total health-program into their mind-set. Their diet or training programs are only "add-ons" that are not coordinated with their long-time established routines.

We often hear from people who quit their fitness programs with the excuse "I had no time…" You have to make your health a priority and give it time!

It's a holistic approach that you should strive for:

- Set goals for your future lifestyle to feel great.
- Celebrate your success with each goal you reach to keep your motivation high.
- Enjoy mental fitness, which keeps you active, alert and enables you to withstand negative stress.
- Stay disciplined in organizing your daily life, focusing on your goals by reserving time for physical activity.
- Enjoy socializing with a group of people who enjoy achieving the same goals as you.

If you stay focused on your goals and are willing to incorporate physical training into your daily or weekly schedule, you will experience how easy and enjoyable this can be.

Eating

If you tried diets, you probably gained the weight back again. You were focused on your diet for a while - but did you really stick to changing your unhealthy eating habits?

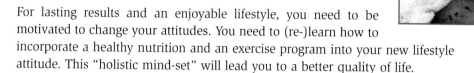

For lasting results and an enjoyable lifestyle, you need to be motivated to change your attitudes. You need to (re-)learn how to incorporate a healthy nutrition and an exercise program into your new lifestyle attitude. This "holistic mind-set" will lead you to a better quality of life.

If you feel overweight, see below for three simple ways how you can check your actual body weight. Find out if you fit into the normal parameters of body weight for the U.S. population in general:

Check your body weight:

Height (without shoes)	Weight (lb) (without clothes)	Weight (lb) (without clothes)
	19 – 34 years	35 years and older
5'1"	97 - 128	108 - 135
5'1"	101 - 132	111 – 143
5'2"	104 - 137	115 – 148
5'3"	107 - 141	119 – 152
5'4"	111 - 146	122 – 157
5'5"	114 - 150	126 – 162
5'6"	118 - 156	130 – 167
5'7"	121 - 160	134 – 172
5'8"	125 - 164	138 – 178
5'9"	129 - 169	142 – 183
5'10"	132 - 174	146 – 186
5'11"	136 - 179	151 – 194
6'0"	140 - 184	155 – 199
6'1"	144 - 189	159 – 205
6'2"	148 - 195	164 - 210

If you do not fit into one of these categories and your body weight is too high, it is time to make changes.

Calculate your Body Mass Index (BMI):

For USA:

BMI = 703 x (Body Weight (lb) / Height(in) x Height (in))

My BMI:..........

Check your BMI:

Weight Categories	Grade of Obesity	BMI kg/m2
Normal	0	20 - 24.9
Overweight	1	25 – 29.9
Obese	2	30 – 39.9
Extrem Obese	3	40 +

If your BMI is 25 and more, it is time to make changes.

Check your waist-to-hip ratio

Another simple method to check your health risk due to body weight, is the 'waist-to-hip-ratio'.

Measure your body shape:

- While standing, measure your waist in inches at its smallest point. Don't suck in your stomach or hold your breath.

- Measure your hips in inches at the widest point.

- Divide your waist measurement in inches by your hip measurement in inches to determine your hip-to-waist ratio.

EXAMPLE:
28 inches (waist) : 40 inches (hip) = 0.70

Your health ratio is at risk, if your ratio is greater than

- 0.80 inches for women
- 0.95 inches for men

If your hip-to-waist ratio is greater, it is time to make changes.

Find out your target calorie level

As I explained in the chapter "Weight Loss", be careful with weight loss programs that promise you will lose five, seven or more pounds per week. This might happen, but you are looking for lasting results. With those programs, your metabolism starts to store fat as soon you end your diet. You begin to gain weight again, often more than you had before.

This is the so-called Yo-Yo Effect.

Health professionals recommend a weight loss of about 1-2 pounds a week over a longer period of time. To improve your metabolic reaction, it is much better to change eating attitudes step-by-step and control your caloric intake.

Learn to chose healthy foods and drinks that have less sugar and fat by checking food labels. You will find many nutritious choices that you enjoy (www.mypyramid.gov). This leads you to more sustainable eating and drinking habits and helps you keep your body weight stable.

Studies suggest the maximum daily calorie intake you need to enable you to lose weight. The recommended daily calorie-intake for men and women of normal weight:

- Women: 1,200 calories per day
- Men: 1,500 calories per day

These are commonly used figures for people who are not working hard physically nor exercising. If you exercise regularly, you can eat more, because you burn more calories and your metabolism adapts. Keep in mind that people differ in how their bodies process food and how they burn calories, but these figures provide a basic orientation.

Activity

Activity is the third component to change to keep a desirable lifestyle.

As described in the chapters 8 and 7 "Improve your Cardio Power" and "Training Plans" start your exercise program now.

Go to these chapters, define your fitness level and start Pole Walking as a beginner, an improved walker or as an advanced walker.

If you are mentally ready to go, follow all these suggestions and you will experience lasting success.

Ten Session
Nordic Pole Walking Program

16

A proven program over ten sessions to improve your cardio power and to strengthen your body muscles:

Class 1 – Introduction & Technique

Class 2 – Cardiovascular & Optimizing Technique

Class 3 – NPW + Strengthening Neck & Shoulder

Class 4 – NPW + Strengthening Back

Class 5 – NPW + Strengthening Legs

Class 6 – NPW + 25% Enhanced Cardiovascular Training

Class 7 – NPW + Advanced Neck & Shoulder Strengthening

Class 8 – NPW + Advanced Strengthening of Back Muscles

Class 9 – NPW + Advanced Strengthening of Legs

Class 10 – NPW - 60 Minutes Continuous Fat Burning

16.1 Class 1 - Introduction & Technique

1. Introduction

Nordic Pole Walking history:

1. Summer training of cross country ski athletes.

2. NPW originally developed in Finland as a common fitness walking program.

3. Spread all over Europe since the year 2000.

4. Is now the fastest growing outdoor wellness sport practiced worldwide.

Nordic Pole Walking health benefits:

Nordic Pole Walking increases all exercise parameters significantly – although it is a low impact exercise!

1. Burns 46% more calories depending on technique & speed.

2. Increases heart and cardiovascular training by 22%.

3. Incorporates more than 90% of all body muscles.

4. Prevents & can eliminate back, shoulder and neck pain.

5. Up to 30% impact on hip and knee joints.

6. Increases production of "positive" hormones.

7. Develops upright body posture.

8. Stress reduction management.

2.   Warm up: (Basic warm up exercises for all classes)

2.1   Breathing exercises

Standing with upright body posture. Poles with stretched-out arms at shoulder height. Turn right and left while deeply exhaling.

Standing upright.
Legs slightly bent.
Stretched arms and
poles overhead.
Bend down while
deeply exhaling.
Raise up while
deeply inhaling.
Keep poles close to
your body.

2.2   Loosening of large joints

Hip and knee joints: Use poles for balance. Swing leg forward and lift knee, then swing back and stretch leg behind you. Change legs.

Stretch right foot in front and rotate ankles in circles. Change feet.

Shoulder joints: Hold poles vertically with stretched-out arms in front of body. Right hand up, left hand down. Swing vertical pole to the right as far back as possible and...

...turn poles upside down, right hand down, left hand up, and swing back to left side. ("kayaking").

2.3 Stretching

Stride position:

1. Stretch calves.

2. Stretch hip flexors.

3. Stretch hamstrings.

4. Stretch quadriceps.

Stretch upper body muscles:

Stretch back muscles

Stretch shoulder-arm muscles

Stretch core muscles

Stretch core muscles

3. Technique & cardiovascular training:

Prior to technique training, instructor demonstrates correct NPW technique so that walkers may visualize it first.

4. Steps to get into Nordic Pole Walking technique:

Step 1: Adjust poles to body height

BODYHEIGHT	WELLNESS-WALKER	ACTIVE-WALKER
< 4'9"	37"	39"
5'2" - 5'4"	39"	41"
5'6"	41"	43"
5'7" - 5'9"	43"	45"
6'1"	45"	47"
6'2" - 6'3"	47"	49"
6'4"	49"	51"
> 6'5"	51"	53"

Active Walker
Wellness Walker - 2"
90° Degree

Step 2: Upright body posture

Poles behind the back. Torso upright. Shoulders relaxed and down.

Step 3: Learn the natural walking technique

Begin with very slow walking with relaxed arms hanging along your sides.

- No arm movement. Concentrate on straight body posture.
- Drag the pole tips on the ground behind you.
- Hands have relaxed contact with Pole grips.

After 100 yards increase walking speed and increase arm swing naturally. Poles will follow the natural arm swing. Hands have still relaxed contact with the grips.

Step 4: "Arms and poles work as the engine"

As soon as you walk with good coordination and rhythm, poles are "pushed" onto the ground with a bit more force and slightly tighter grip. Automatically, the walking speed increases. While swinging the arm forward, the Pole tip is lifted slightly. No dragging any more.

Walk in intervals:

100 yards with more force to the poles.

100 yards with less force to the poles.

You recognize that the "power of the poles" is propelling you forward.

Step 5: Engaging your upper body muscles

Push backwards:
While putting more force on the poles, the poles are pushed backwards as far as the given surface allows (sand, clay, grass, asphalt). Hands swing behind the hip and will be opened (relaxed) slightly at the end of the back swing.

Shoulder rotation:
While walking in a good rhythm, the shoulders actively begin rotating forward and backward, coordinating with the walking rhythm to engage the core and back muscles.

Step 6: Cool down
The Cool Down is practiced in the opposite sequence as the Warm up

- Strengthening exercises (if appropriate)
- Stretching exercises
- Loosening exercises (relaxing exercises)
- Breathing exercises

16.2 Class 2 – Cardiovascular & Optimizing Technique

Part 1. Warm-up

- Breathing exercises
- Loosening exercises
- Stretching exercises

Part 2. Cardio training

- Repetition of first 6 technique steps
- 20 minutes Pole Walking
- Medium speed
- Instructor corrects technique
- 5 minutes stretching exercises
- 20 minutes Pole Walking with intervals about every 5 minutes with more and less force to the poles

Part 3. Cool down

- Strengthening exercises (if appropriate)
- Stretching exercises
- Loosening exercises (relaxing exercises)
- Breathing exercises

16.3   Class 3 – Nordic Pole Walking + Strengthening Neck & Shoulder

Part 1. Warm-up

- Breathing
- Loosening
- Stretching
- Shoulders
- Core muscles
- Back
- Neck

Part 2. Training

1. 25 minutes Pole Walking

2. 10 minutes strengthening neck & shoulders

3. Overhead push ups with poles, 20x

4. Overhead push ups with poles while pulling hands apart, 20x (isometric/ dynamic)
Same, but pushing hands together, 20x

5. Isometric exercises:

- Hold poles with stretched-out arms in front of chest at shoulder height. Pull hands apart with tight grip in same position. Count to 15.
  Same exercise, pushing hands together. Count to 15.

- Hold poles vertically behind the back (see picture). Pull hands up and down at the same time. First set right hand up, second set left hand up. Count to 15 per set.

- Poles overhead. Pull apart. Count to 15.

- Poles overhead. Push together. Count to 15.

6. 20 minutes Pole Walk.

Part 3. Cool down

- Strengthening exercises (if appropriate)

- Stretching exercises

- Loosening exercises (relaxing exercises)

- Breathing exercises

16.4 Class 4 – Nordic Pole Walking + Strengthening Back

Part 1. Warm-up

- Breathing

- Mobilizing joints

- Stretching

Part 2. Training

1. 25 minutes Pole Walking

2. 10 minutes strengthening back muscles

3. Poles overhead with stretched arms, bending forward, 15x

4. Both poles in front for balance. In slow motion, stretch left leg backward, then swing forward with bent knee up toward chest. 15x.

Same with right leg. 15x.

5. Left pole in front for balance. Body weight on right leg. Stretch left leg backward and at the same time, stretch right arm forward and up. 15x.

Change sides. Same exercise 15x.

6. Balance body weight on right leg. Both hands hold pole in front of quadriceps. Lift poles forward and up and stretch left leg backward. 15x.

Same exercise with body weight on left leg. 15x.

7. Stretch your back muscles for relaxation.

8. 20 minutes of Pole Walking.

Part 3. Cool down

- Strengthening exercises (if appropriate)
- Stretching exercises
- Loosening exercises (relaxing exercises)
- Breathing exercises

16.5 Class 5 – Nordic Pole Walking + Strengthening Legs

Part 1. Warm-up

- Breathing
- Loosening joints
- Stretching
- Plus 5 squats in different positions

Part 2. Training

1. 30 minutes Pole Walking

2. Strengthening leg muscles

- Calves: Use poles for balance. Body weight on right leg. Raise heels. 15x. Same with other leg. 15x.

- Quadriceps: Feet shoulder-width apart. Use poles for balance. Sit down in a virtual chair. 15x.

- Stride position. Right foot in front. Use poles for balance. "Kneel" down on left knee and raise up. 10x.
  Then left foot in front. 10x.

3. 20 minutes Pole Walking

Part 3. Cool down

For stretching: Focus on stretching for quadriceps, calves after strengthening exercises.

16.6 Class 6 – Nordic Pole Walking + 25% Enhanced Cardiovascular Training

Part 1. Warm up

- Breathing
- Loosening joints
- Stretching
- Focus on calves, hamstrings, quadriceps

Part 2. Training

1. 15 minutes Pole Walking:
   Speed: 60% - 65% of PRmax.
   After 15 minutes: count heart beats/min.

2. 15 minutes walking faster:
   Speed: 75% - 80% of PRmax.
   After 15 minutes: count heart beats/min.

3. Break for stretching.

4. 15 minutes interval walking:
   2 minutes fast with more force to the poles.
   2 minutes slow walking.
   4 intervals.

- 10 minutes comfortable speed:
  Speed: 60% - 65% of PRmax.

Part 3. Cool down

- Strengthening exercises (if appropriate)
- Stretching exercises
- Loosening exercises (relaxing exercises)
- Breathing exercises

16.7 Class 7 – Nordic Pole Walking + Advanced Neck & Shoulder Strengthening

Part 1. Warm-up

- Breathing
- Loosening: Focus on neck & shoulder
- Stretching

Part 2. Training

1. 30 minutes Pole Walking.
   Speed: 60% - 65% of max heart rate

2. Strengthening neck & shoulder: (Exercises see Class 4)

3. Additional partner exercises:

- 2 partners face-to-face in stride position. Each partner holds the other end of both poles. One partner tries to "push" the other.

- Push ups:
  Partner 1 kneels down. Poles behind the neck. Grip shoulder width apart.
  Partner 2, standing behind partner 1, pushes down onto the poles from above providing resistance while partner 1 pushes the poles upward.

10 push ups. Then change of partner position. 2 sets for both partners.

- Latissimus pulls:
  Partner 1 kneels down. Poles with stretched arms overhead.
  Partner 2, standing behind partner 1, grips the poles from underneath and pushes upward, providing resistance while partner 1 pulls the poles down behind head.

10x pulls. Then partners change position. 2 sets per position.

4. 20 Minutes Pole Walking.

Part 3. Cool down

Focus on cool down: stretch and relax neck and shoulder muscles.

16.8 Class 8 – Nordic Pole Walking +
Advanced Strengthening of Back Muscles

Part 1. Warm-up

- Breathing
- Loosening
- Stretching

Part 2. Training

1. 30 minutes Pole Walking. Speed 60% - 65% of PRmax.

2. Strengthening neck & shoulder:
- All Exercises as in Class 3.
- Every Exercise 15 repetitions for 3 sets.

4. 20 minutes Pole Walking. Speed: 60% - 65% of PRmax.

Part 3. Cool down

Focus: Relax neck & shoulder muscles.

16.9 Class 9 – Nordic Pole Walking + Advanced Strengthening of Legs

Part 1. Warm-up

- Breathing
- Loosening
- Stretching: Focus on leg muscles

Part 2. Training

1. 30 minutes Pole Walking. Speed: 60% - 65% of PRmax.

2. Strengthening legs:
- All exercises from Class 5 with more repetitions
- All exercises 10 repetitions for 3 sets

3. 20 minutes Pole Walking. Speed: 60% - 65% of PRmax.

Part 3. Cool down

Focus: Stretching/relaxing leg muscles.

16.10 Class 10 – Nordic Pole Walking – 60 Minutes Continuous Fat Burning

Part 1. Warm-up

- Breathing
- Loosening
- Stretching

Part 2. Training

1. 20 minutes Pole Walking. Speed: 60% - 65% of PRmax.

2. 20 minutes Pole Walking. Speed: 75% of PRmax.

3. 20 minutes PoleWalking. Speed: 60% - 65% PRmax.

Part 3. Cool down

Focus on stretching and breathing.

17 Training Plans for Your Success

When it is your goal to improve your physical performance step-by-step and with guaranteed success, a systematic built-up training plan is crucial.

This book offers training plans to achieve four fitness-levels: from the very beginner, to improved walker, to advanced and race walker. You choose how far you want to go.

Before starting a systematic training, check your actual fitness level:

1. Check your **health status** with the Fitness Activity Readiness Questionnaire (American Heart Association).

2. Check your **fitness level** with the Fitness Calculator to help you determine your starting point at the following training plans. From there, you can start your training systematically to improve your performance according to the suggested training plans.

Whether you are ...

A beginner ...

An improved walker ...

An advanced walker ...

A race walker ...

17.1   Fitness Activity Readiness Questionnaire

(Source: American Heart Association)

Answer this questionnaire before you start training!	YES	NO
• I have a heart condition and my healthcare professional recommends only medically supervised physical activity.	....	....
• During or right after I exercise, I often have pain or pressure in my neck, left shoulder, or arm.	....	....
• I have developed chest pain within the last month.	....	....
• I tend to lose consciousness or fall over, due to dizziness.	....	....
• I become extremely breathless after mild exertion.	....	....
• My healthcare provider recommends that I take medicine for high blood pressure.	....	....
• I have bone or joint problems that limit my ability to do moderately-intense physical activity.	....	....
• I have a medical condition or other physical reason not mentioned here that might need special attention in an exercise program.	....	....
• I am pregnant and my healthcare professional has not given me the OK to be physically active.	....	....
• I am over 50, haven't been physically active and I am planning a vigorous exercise program.	....	....

If you selected one or more YES, it's important that you see your healthcare professional before you START.
(American Heart Association)

17.2 Fitness Calculator – Check your Fitness Level

Questions	Evaluate your fitness	Points	Insert your points
1. Are you physically active?	None	0	
	Low	1	
	Medium	2	
	High	3	
2. How intense is your training?	Low	1	
	Medium	2	
	High	3	
	Exhausting	4	
3. How many training sessions per week?	1x	1	
	2x	2	
	3x	3	
	more	4	
4. How many minutes is one training session?	Less 20 Min.	1	
	20-40 Min.	2	
	more	3	

CLASSIFICATION:			Total:
→ 4 points: Beginner			
5-8 points: Improved			
9-11 points: Advanced			
12 ore more: Performance			

If you go to www.gnpwalking.com the calculation is done automatically and you will be directed to suggested training plans, adjusted to your fitness level.

17.3 Fitness Calculator Classification

Less than 4 points:

Go to the training plan: "Beginner/Basic Walker"

You are pretty passive with your physical activities.
You should start your training NOW!

Start with 2 x 1.5 miles/training (= approx. 20 min/mile).
This is approximately 30 minutes per training session.

Try following our training schedule and improving your walking-endurance step by step. You will be able to walk 9.5 miles per week = 36 miles per month) easily after only 12 weeks.

5 – 8 points:

Go to the training plan: "Improved Walker"

You are not engaging in enough physical training. You could be more active. Start with 2 miles/ training session. Follow our training plan. After 4 weeks you will be able to walk up to 50 miles/ month.

9 – 11 points:

Go to the training plan: "Advanced Walker"

Your training activity is pretty well-established. However, you can do more. Enhance your training to 3 x 60 minutes per week.
See training plan.

12 points and more:

Go to the training plan: "Performance Walker"

Your training performance is excellent.
Listen to your body's signals – do not exhaust yourself.
If you are motivated to participate in 5K, 10K, Half Marathon or Marathon challenges, see the training plan.

17.4 How to Use the Basic Training Plans

This Basic Training Plan takes you to your next fitness level: From "Beginner" to "Improved Walker," to "Advanced Walker" and finally to "Performance Walker."

Other than your general fitness training, the schedules prepare you for 5K, 10K, Half-Marathon and Marathon Walks – if you like.

The Basic Training Plans were developed through years of experience in training walkers. Although these schedules are not tailored to each individual as published here, they will work to your satisfaction.

Read the instructions to learn how easy it is to adjust the training schedules to your individual fitness level.

Nordic Pole Walking USA LLC provides a website, where you can determine your personal goals and monitor and evaluate miles walked, calories burned, weight loss, blood pressure, daily blood sugar measurement for diabetics and performance:

www.GNPWalking.com.

"Enjoy Achieving Your Goals" - Your Satisfaction - Your Trophy

This website provides a Fitness Calculator (chapter 17.2), which directs you to training schedules according to your actual fitness level. It also allows tracking your training data and evaluating your miles, calories and weight loss progress.

Fitness Level 1: "Basic Walker" (up to NPW 5K)

If you have not been physically exercising for many years, consult the "Activity Readiness Questionnaire." If you have answered "YES" to any of the questions, consult your health professional before you begin Nordic Pole Walking.

Prepare yourself mentally to commit to the program. Begin by walking one 20 minute mile 2 days per week. At the end of the first month you will have achieved 10 miles.

If you feel like you can easily walk additional miles, switch to a weekly program slowly increasing your mileage to achieve your goal of 9 miles per week.

Once achieved, proceed to the Nordic Pole Walking Training Schedule for "Improved Walkers" at which time you will be ready to participate in your first 5K (charity) walk.

Don't become over-motivated and too competitive as you participate in your first 5K walk. Enjoy the event with your friends and walk at a moderate pace.

Fitness Level: "Improved Walker" (up to NPW 10K)

If you are used to performing a regular physical training at least twice a week and you now feel very comfortable Pole Walking for 3 or 4 miles, it is time to start the Training Schedule for "Improved Walkers."

When you achieve your goal of walking 10 miles per week at about 19 minutes per mile, proceed to the next week of the Nordic Pole Walking Training Schedule. Now you have reached a good fitness level.

If you like, participate in a 10K (charity) walk with your poles.
Once you are able to walk 15 miles per week, you are ready to finish a 10K (charity) walk. For your first 10K don't be too ambitious, just finish and evaluate the experience you had. The next time you walk a 10K, you might try racing and strive to better your walking time.

When you have achieved an average of 15 miles per week and you are ready to go to the next level, go to the Nordic Pole Walking Training Schedule for "Advanced Walkers". This training schedule lifts you to a higher fitness level and when you follow the Basic Training Plan it prepares you for a Nordic Pole Walking Half-Marathon.

Fitness Level: "Advanced Walker" (up to NPW Half-Marathon)

To start preparation for NPW Half-Marathons, you should be able to pole-walk at least 3 times a week with an average mileage of 15 miles per week.

Walk at a speed of 18 minutes per mile.
Follow month 1 – 6 and you will be ready for a NPW Half-Marathon.

Three weeks before your NPW Half Marathon, test yourself at a mileage that comes close to the Half-Marathon distance.

2 weeks before the race, your training mileage should decrease so that you will be strong for the race.

Fitness Level: "Performance Walker" (up to NPW Marathon)

To start preparation for a NPW Marathon, you should be used to a regular NPW training of at least about 20 miles per week for more than 6 months.

Walk at a speed of 15 to 17 minutes per mile, depending on your individual condition. Then follow the Nordic Pole Walking Training Schedule for another 6 months. 5 weeks before your race, test yourself with walking about 20 miles and then decrease the mileage to be strong and well-prepared for your NPW Marathon.

Applaud Yourself!

17.5 BEGINNER / BASIC WALKER

	YOUR GOAL Total/Week		YOUR GOAL Kcal/Mile		M T W TH F Sat Sun	Actually Done Per Week Miles	Actually Done Per Week Kcal
Mile/Week							
0:20:00			150				
1st Month	Miles	Minutes					
1	2.5	0:50:00	375				
2	2.5	0:50:00	375				
3	2.5	0:50:00	375				
4	2.5	0:50:00	375				
2nd Month	10	3:20:00	1500				
5	3.5	1:10:00	525				
6	3.5	1:10:00	525				
7	3.5	1:10:00	525				
8	3.5	1:10:00	525				
3rd Month	14	4:40:00	2100				
9	5	1:40:00	750				
10	5	1:40:00	750				
11	5	1:40:00	750				
12	5	1:40:00	750				
	20	6:40:00	3000				
4th Month							
13	5	1:40:00	750				
14	5	1:40:00	750				
15	5	1:40:00	750				
16	5	1:40:00	750				
5th Month	20	6:40:00	3.000				
17	7	2:20:00	1050				
18	7	2:20:00	1050				
19	7	2:20:00	1050				
20	7	2:20:00	1050				
6th Month	28	9:20:00	4200				
21	9	3:00:00	1350				
22	9	3:00:00	1350				
23	9	3:00:00	1350				
24	9	3:00:00	1350				
	36	12:00:00	5400				

17.6 IMPROVED WALKER (up to 10K)

Mile/Week	YOUR GOAL Total/Week		YOUR GOAL Kcal/Mile	Protocol	M	T	W	TH	F	Sat	Sun	Actually Done Per Week Miles	Actually Done Per Week Kcal
0:19:00			150	Protocol									
1st Month	Miles	Minutes			M	T	W	TH	F	Sat	Sun	Miles	Kcal
1	10	3:10:00	1500										
2	10	3:10:00	1500										
3	10	3:10:00	1500										
4	10	3:10:00	1500										
2nd Month	40	12:40:00	6000										
5	11	3:29:00	1650										
6	11	3:29:00	1650										
7	11	3:29:00	1650										
8	11	3:29:00	1650										
3rd Month	44	13:56:00	6600										
9	12	3:48:00	1800										
10	12	3:48:00	1800										
11	12	3:48:00	1800										
12	12	3:48:00	1800										
	48	15:12:00	7200										
4th Month													
13	13	4:07:00	1950										
14	13	4:07:00	1950										
15	13	4:07:00	1950										
16	13	4:07:00	1950										
5th Month	52	16:28:00	7.800										
17	14	4:26:00	2100										
18	14	4:26:00	2100										
19	14	4:26:00	2100										
20	14	4:26:00	2100										
6th Month	56	17:44:00	8400										
21	15	4:45:00	2250										
22	15	4:45:00	2250										
23	15	4:45:00	2250										
24	15	4:45:00	2250										
	60	19:00:00	9000										

17.7 ADVANCED WALKER (up to Half Marathon)

Mile/Week	YOUR GOAL Total/Week		YOUR GOAL Kcal/Mile									Actually Done Per Week	Actually Done Per Week
0:18:00			150										
1st Month	Miles	Minutes		M	T	W	TH	F	Sat	Sun		Miles	Kcal
1	16	4:48:00	2400										
2	16	4:48:00	2400										
3	16	4:48:00	2400										
4	16	3:10:00	2400										
2nd Month	64	17:34:00	9600										
5	17	5:06:00	2550										
6	17	3:29:00	2550										
7	17	5:06:00	2550										
8	17	5:06:00	2550										
3rd Month	68	18:47:00	10200										
9	18	5:24:00	2700										
10	18	5:24:00	2700										
11	18	5:24:00	2700										
12	18	5:24:00	2700										
	72	21:36:00	10800										
4th Month													
13	19	5:42:00	2850										
14	19	5:42:00	2850										
15	19	5:42:00	2850										
16	19	5:42:00	2850										
5th Month	76	22:48:00	11.400										
17	20	6:00:00	3000										
18	20	6:00:00	3000										
19	20	6:00:00	3000										
20	20	6:00:00	3000										
6th Month	80	0:00:00	12000										
21	21	6:18:00	3150										
22	21	6:18:00	3150										
23	21	6:18:00	3150										
24	21	6:18:00	3150										
	84	1:12:00	12600										

17.8 PERFORMANCE WALKER (up to Marathon)

Mile/Week	YOUR Goal Total/Week		YOUR Goal Kcal/Mile		M	T	W	TH	F	Sat	Sun	Actually Done Per Week Miles	Actually Done Per Week Kcal
0:17:00			150										
1st Month	Miles	Minutes											
1	20	5:40:00	3000										
2	22	6:14:00	3300										
3	24	6:48:00	3600										
4	26	3:10:00	3900										
2nd Month	92	21:52:00	13800										
5	22	6:14:00	3300										
6	24	6:14:00	3600										
7	26	7:22:00	3900										
8	28	7:56:00	4200										
3rd Month	100	3:46:00	15000										
9	24	6:48:00	3600										
10	26	7:22:00	3900										
11	28	7:56:00	4200										
12	30	8:30:00	4500										
	108	6:36:00	16200										
4th Month													
13	24	6:48:00	3600										
14	28	7:56:00	4200										
15	32	9:04:00	4800										
16	36	10:12:00	5400										
5th Month	120	10:00:00	18.000										
17	26	7:22:00	3900										
18	30	8:30:00	4500										
19	34	9:38:00	5100										
20	38	10:46:00	5700										
6th Month	128	12:16:00	19200										
21	26	7:22:00	3900										
22	26	7:22:00	3900										
23	22	6:14:00	3300										
24	26	7:22:00	3900										
	100	4:20:00	15000										

17.9 Advice in Handling the Training Plan for Beginners/Basic Walkers

First: Fill out the Fitness Calculator

The Fitness Calculator directs you to the training level (Basic Walker, Improved Walker, Advanced Walker, Performance Walker).

Second: Use your own records, if applicable

If you have your own records about training miles, go the training level you think will fit your fitness level.

Third: Getting started as a beginner

If you are starting Pole Walking right from the beginning go to the "Basic Walker" training plan and start with week No. 1 (2.5 miles per week). It is recommended that you split this amount of weekly miles into 2 walking sessions. Your speed should be about 20 minutes per mile. This feels comfortable and you can enjoy Pole Walking and improve your technique. Follow the training plan, which leads you carefully and step-by-step to higher performance levels.

Fifth: Going to higher levels

If you feel comfortable and have no soreness after Pole Walking and you want to walk more miles per week, "jump" to a weekly mileage you think you think you would be able to do without getting sore and start from there. Follow the increase of miles as suggested in the training plan.

Sixth: Increase your weekly mileage

Once you have found your walking routine as a beginner, do not increase your weekly mileage more than 2 miles per week. A body that hasn't exercised for years needs time to adjust to the training. Your joints (cartiledge and tendons) need 7 times longer to adjust to training than your cardio system. We often see that beginners increase pace and distance too fast, which can result in injuries of your feet, ankles, knees and hips. Take your time when you are a beginner before increasing your mileage too much.

17.10 Training Advice for Performance Walkers in Preparation for a Marathon

Each training session begins with a 10-15 minute warm-up:
- *Breathing deeply*
- *Loosening of joints: ankle, knee, hip and shoulder joints*
- *Easy stretching*
- *10 minutes of comfortable walking*

One day of speed intervals:

On days you walk shorter distances (4 miles), practice speed by doing short intervals at a faster pace, then interrupt with a comfortable pace in between intervals. Start walking with 1 minute faster and 2 minutes slower. Step by step build up to 2 minutes of fast and 1 minute of slow intervals.

One day faster pace:

Walk a steady pace at a faster tempo on a day with a walking distance of 4-5 miles. Push yourself, but choose a pace which allows you to walk the total distance at the same speed.

One long distance day:

This day prepares you to walk at a speed a little faster than easy for the marathon distance (see training plan for Performance Walkers). Choose a weekend day to have time to rest on that day and to prepare your biorhythm for long distance for a weekend race. The closer you come to the marathon day, chose a speed you will walk at the marathon.

Technique day:

On one day with a comfortable walking pace, concentrate on your technique and a perfect form.

Cross training:

Use the technique day to incorporate exercises for strengthening and flexibility. Incorporate squats (3 sets x 15-25 squats) and exercise to strengthen you back and core muscles in the middle of your training distance.

Off-days:

Take at least one day off to regenerate your body. The best rest day is after the long distance day.

18 Most Frequently Asked Questions about Nordic Pole Walking:

1. *What equipment do I need?*
   You need a pair of Nordic poles and sneakers – and adequate clothing according to your local climate. Then, you are ready to go.

2. *Where can I Nordic Pole Walk?*
   Nordic Pole Walking can be performed on literally any surface, just about everywhere. On hard surface (pavement) you will use the rubber tips. On clay, sand, soil and grass you will remove the rubber tips.

3. *Which parts of my body are being trained/exercised?*
   Nordic Pole Walking trains and exercises all body muscles, the cardiovascular system and also burns calories—all in ONE exercise.

4. *How does the training affect my upper body?*
   Nordic Pole Walking involves approximately 90% of your muscles and especially engages your upper body and arm muscles.

5. *Is Nordic Pole Walking good for cardiovascular training, too?*
   Nordic Pole Walking increases your heart rate by approximately 15 beats per minute.

6. *How much does Nordic Pole Walking increase energy consumption?*
   Nordic Pole Walking increases your energy consumption by an average of 20%.

7. *How does Nordic Pole Walking lead to an erect body posture?*
   Nordic Pole Walking leads to stabilization off the spinal musculature and upright body posture by the very nature of the exercises.

8. *How many calories are burned in an hour of Nordic Pole Walking?*
   Nordic Pole Walking increases burning of calories by up to 46% (up to 900 calories per hour compared with 280 calories per hour for walking without poles or 600 calories when jogging without poles).

9. *Is Nordic Pole Walking good for my neck and shoulder mobility?*
   Nordic Pole Walking significantly increases the lateral mobility of your neck and spine.

10. *Is there less impact to the joints than with jogging or running?*
    Nordic Pole Walking reduces the impact on your knee and hip joints by 30%.

11. *Does Nordic Pole Walking help reduce pain?*
    Nordic Pole Walking mitigates pain and muscle tension in the neck, shoulder and back regions.

12. *What is the correct length of the poles I should be using?*
    The correct length of the poles is 65% of your body height.

13. *Should I use adjustable or non-adjustable poles?*
    Beginners should start with adjustable Nordic poles.

14. *What is the difference between Nordic Walking Poles and ski and/or hiking poles?*
    The hand loops on Nordic poles are designed to perform the correct technique and to achieve the most benefit for the upper body muscles. You cannot use hiking or ski poles for Nordic Pole Walking because they are designed for different purposes.

Only by practicing a good Nordic Pole Walking technique can you achieve all of the health benefits described.

19 Literature Sources

Ainsworth, B.E., Haskell, W.L., A.S. Jacobs, D.R., H.J. Sallis, J.F. Pfaffenberger, RS.(1993). Compendium of Physical Activities: Classification of energy cost of human physical activities. Medicine and Science in Sports and Exercise, 15:1 71-80.

American College of Sports Medicine (1995): Guidelines for graded exercise testing and prescription. 5th issue, Philadelphia.

Arent, S.W., Rogers, T., Landers, D.M. (2001): Mental Health and Physical Activity. The effects of physical activity on selected mental health variables: Determining causation. Sportwissenschaft 2001, 31:239 – 254.

Berg, A., Delbert, P., Berg, A., Jr, Koenig, D., Dickhut, H.H.(2204): Current views on the importance of physical activity. Muenchener Medizinische Wochenschrift, Fortschritt der Medizin,146:27-30.

Blair, S.N., Brodney,S. (1999): Effects and physical inactivity and obesity on mortality: current evidence and research issues. In: Medicine and Science in Sports and Exercise 1999, 31: 646 – 662.

Blair, S.R., Conelly, J.C. (1996): How much physical activity should we do? The case of moderate amounts and intensities of physical activity. In: Research Quarterly for Exercise and Sport, 1996, 67: 193 – 205.

Blair, S.N., Kohl, H.W., Pfaffenberger, R.S., Clark, D.C., Cooper, K.H., Gibbons, L.W. (1989): Physical fitness and all-cause mortality. A prospective study of healthy men and women. In: Journal of American Medical Association 1989, 262:2395 – 2401.

Bouchard, C. (2001): Dose-response concerning physical activity and health: an evidence-based symposium. Medicine and Science in Sport and Exercises, 2001:33.

Bouchard, C., Shepard R. (1994): Physical activity, fitness and health. The model and key concepts. In: Bouchard, C., Shepard, R., Stephens, T. (eds). Physical activity, fitness and health. Campaign: Human-Kinetics 1994:77 -88.

Crews, D.J., Landers, D.M. (1987): A meta-analytic review of aerobic fitness and reactivity to psycho-social stressors. In: Medicine and Science in Sports and Exercise, 1987, 19:114 – 120.

Dishman, R.K., Buckworth, J. (1996): Increasing physical activity: A quantitative synthesis. In: Medicine and Science in Sports and Exercise 1996, 28:706 – 719.

Dunn, A.L., Blair, S.N. (2002): Translating evidence-based physical activity interventions into practice. The 2010 challenge. In: American Journal of Preventive Medicine, 2002, 4: 221 – 225.

Franz, A., Esser, T., Luecke, S., Roth, R., Brueggemann, G.P.(2006): Experimental comparison of the knee joint loading during Nordic walking and walking. Journal of Biomechanics, 39, Supp.1 185.

Gruenberg, C., Joellenbeck, T., Leyser, D., Classen, C. (2006): Field testing to determine biomechanical laoding of lower limb during nordic walking versus walking – comparison between nordic walking instructors and experienced nordic walkers. Journal of Biomechanics, 39 Suppl.1 186.

Hagen, M., Henning, E.M., Stieldorf, P.(2006): Belastungsgroessen beim Nordic Walking im Vergleich zum Laufen. E-Journal Bewegung und Training.

Hoeltke, V., Steuer, M., Joens, H., Krakor, S., Steinacker, T., & Jacob, E. (2005): Walking versus Nordic Walking II – Belastungsparameter im Vergleich. Deutsche Zeitschrift fuer Sportmedizin, 56:7/8:243.

Hollmann, W., Hettinger, T. (2000): Sports Medicine: Basis for work, training and preventive medicine. 4th Suppl., Schattauer, Stuttgart 2000.

Jacobsen, B.H., Kapoluek, J., Smith, D.B. (2005): Load carriage force production comparison between standard and anti-shock trekking poles. The sports journal, 8.3, http://the sportjournal.org/2005Journal/Vol8-No3/Jacobson.asp (August 2006).

Joellenbeck, T., Leyser, D., Gruenberg, C.(2006): Nordic Walking – A field of biomechanical loading of the lower extremities. Isokinetics and Exercises 14.2:127.

Jolliffe, J.A., Rees, K., Taylor, R.S., Thompson, D., Oldridge, N., Ebrahim, S.(2001): Exercise-based rehabilitation for coronary heart disease (Cochrane Review). Issue 1. Update Sotftware: Cochrane library, Oxford, 2001.

Kohl, H.W. (2001): Physical activity and cardiovascular disease: Evidence for dose response. In: Medicine and Science in Sport and Exercise 2001, 33:472 – 483.

McDonald, D.G., Hodgon, J.A. (1991): Psychological effects of aerobic fitness fitness training. In: Research and theory. Springer, New York, 1991.

Mart, B., Martin, B.W., (2001): Physical activity to optimize health and quality of life. In: Therapeutische Umschau 2001, 58:189 – 195.

Mommert-Jauch, P. (2007): Gesund mit Nordic Walking. BLV Buchverlag, Muenchen, 2007.

Mommert-Jauch, P., Butz, M., Edel, K., Boes, K.(2007): Nordic Walking bei Diabetes und Metabolischem Syndrom. Verlag Haug, Stuttgart, 2007.

Pate, R.R., Pratt, M., Blair, S.N., Haskell, W., Macera, D., Bouchard, C., Buchner, D. et. al. (1995): Physical activity and public health: A recommendation from the centers for disease control and prevention and the American College of Sports Medicine. In: Journal of the American Medical Association 1995, 273: 402 – 407.

Perlmutter, D. (2004): The Better Brain Book, The Berkley Publishing Group, New York, USA.

Pfaffenberger, R.S., Hyde, R.T., Wing, A.L., Hsieh, C.C. (1984); Physical activity, all cause mortally, and longevity of college alumni. New England Journal of Medicine 314: 605 – 613.

Pfeifer, K. (2004): Praevention von Erkrankungen des Bewegungsapparates – Evidenzbasierung. In: Bewegungstherapie und Gesundheitssport 2004, 20:68 – 69.

Phillips, W.T., Pruitt, L.A., King, A.C. (1996): Lifestyle activity. Current recommendations. In: Sports Medicine 1996, 22: 1 – 7.

Pocari, J.P., Hendrickson, T.L., Walter, P.R., Terry, L. & Walsco, G. (1997): The physiological response to walking with and without power poles on treadmill exercise. Research Quarterly for Exercise and Sport, 68(2):161 – 166.

Push, H. (2005): Nordic Walking als Osteoporosetherapie – erste Resultate. In" Kongressband zum 3. Internationalen Nordic Walking Kongress , Bad Tatzmann dorf.

Rockhill, B., Willet, W.C., Manson, J.E., Leitzmann, M.F., Stampfer, M.J., Hunter, D.J., Colditz, G.A. (2001): Physical activity and mortality: A prospective study among women. In: American Journal of Public Health 2001, 91: 578 – 583.

Rothenbacher, D., Hoffmeister, A., Brenner, H., Koenig, W. (2003): Physical activity, coronary heart disease, and inflammatory responses. In: Archives of Internal Medicine 2003, 163:1200 – 1205.

Ruetten, A., Abu-Omar, K. (2003): Praevention durch Bewegung. Zur Evidenzbasierung von Interventionen zur Foerderung koerperlicher Aktivitaet. In: Zeitschrift fuer Gesundheitswissenschaften 2003, 2:229 – 246.

Rusack, P., Ahrens, U., Thorwesten, L., Voelker, K., (2005): Vergleich der kardiopulmonalen und metabolischen Belastungscharakteristik des Walkings und Nordic Walkings – Konsequenzen fuer die Trainingssteuerung. Deutsche Zeitschrift fuer Sportmedizin, 56:7/8, 253.

Saltin, B., Helge, J.W. (2000): Skeleton musculature, physical activity and health. In: Orthopaede 2000, 29: 941 – 947.

Schlicht, W., Kanning, M., Boes, K. (2003): Psycho-social interventions to influence the secondary risk factor unactivity. In: Jordan, J., Barde, B., Zeier, A.M. (Hrsg.). Expertise for the Status- and Consensus Conference in Psycho-Cardiology 2003.

Schwameder, H., Roithner, R., Mueller, E., Niessen, W., Raschner, C. (1999): Knee joint forces during downhill walking with hiking poles. Journal of Sports Sciences, 17:969 – 978.

Schwameder, H. (2006): Lower extremity joint loading in level and graded walking. Journal of Biomechanics, 39, Suppl. 1:185.

Thorwesten, L., Overhaus, N., Voelker, K. (2005): Ground reaction forces in Nordic Walking and Walking. In: Schwameder, H., Strutzenberger, G., Fastenbauer, V., Lindinger, S., Mueller, E. (Rds.): Proceedings of the XXIV. International Symposium on Biomechanics in Sports; 628.

Voelker, K., Rusack, P., Ahrens, U., Thorwesten, L. (2005): Effects of an eight-week Nordic Walking training on endurance and strength development of untrained people. Deutsche Zeitschrift fuer Sportmedizin, 56:7/8:255.

Von Stengel, S., Bartosch, H. (2004): Nordic Walking. Verlag Copress, Muenchen 2004.

Wilson, J., Torry, M.R., Decker, M.J., Kernozek, T.,Steadman, J.R. (2001): Effects of walking poles on lower extremity gait mechanics. Medicine & Science in Sports & Exercise, 1:142 – 147.

Internet Resources

National Osteoporosis Foundation (NOF). Washington, DC. www.NOF.org.

American Heart Association. www.americanheart.com

Age Matters. www.age-matters.org.

American Diabetes Association. www.diabetes.org.

University of Pittsburgh Medical Center. www.upmc.com.

United States Department of Agriculture (USDA), www.MyPyramid.gov.

The Author

Dr. Klaus D. Schwanbeck

Education

1972   Master of Physical Education and Training Sciences, Johannes Gutenberg University, Mainz, Germany.

1978   Ph.D. in System Theory and Communication, Technical University Berlin and University Bayreuth, Germany.

Professional Experience

1972   National Head Coach, Germany's National Track and Field Team, Mainz, Germany.

1980   General Manager, Sports Academy Berlin, Germany.
Vice-President, Germany's National Instructor Licensing Committee.
Founder and Developer of Nationwide Sports and Health Programs in Germany.

1990   General Manager and Partner of a leading Public Relations and Marketing Agency, Koob & Partner, Muehlheim/R, Germany.

1995   Founder and CEO, Health Academy Berlin, Germany.
Marketing Counselor to Germany's Health Insurance Companies, Medical Boards and Fitness Industry.

2000   Founder of the "German Preventive Health Network," Berlin, Germany.

2006   President and CEO, Nordic Pole Walking USA LLC, Naples, FL, USA.

Photo & Illustration Credits

Cover Photo: Imago
Cover Design: Jens Vogelsang
Photos: www.morguefile.com
                www.pixelio.de
                www.sxc.hu
                www.dreamstime.com
                POLAR Electro GmbH Germany (S. 20, 103)

Jeff & Barbara Galloway
**Women's Complete
Guide to Walking**

232 pages, full-color print
60 color photos
Paperback, 6^1/$_2$" x 9^1/$_4$"
ISBN: 978-1-84126-218-5
$ 16.95 US
£ 12.95 UK/€ 16.95

This book provides practical information on issues that are specific to women. There is also information on fatburning, day-by-day schedules to get you into shape, motivation tips, and inspirational stories of women who have worked through major challenges in their lives, empowered by exercise. The nutrition section offers specific eating suggestions, with advice from highly recognized sports nutritionist Nancy Clark, RD. The information presented in this book is accessible and inspirational.

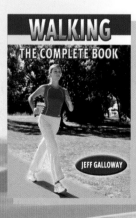

Jeff Galloway
Walking – The Complete Book

216 pages, full-color print
48 photos, 16 illustrations
Paperback, 5^3/$_4$" x 8^1/$_4$"
ISBN: 978-1-84126-170-6
$ 17.95 US
£ 12.95 UK/€ 16.95

This book will motivate you to get moving, avoid aches and pains, and enjoy a more energetic life. Whether you are just starting to walk around the block, or have been active for years, "Walking – The Complete Book" has a world of information that will make you want to walk every day, as it helps you improve the experience. This book explains how to keep moving forward – for life.